Life's
Mountains

Life's Mountains

Cheryl L. Broyles

CONTENTS

ACKNOWLEDGMENTS

After climbing Mount Shasta, I was inspired to write a book. I sat down and drafted an outline, but didn't know where to go from there.

A friend with brain tumor, Ed, told me about the Klamath Writers' Guild. I finally attended a guild meeting and brought my first draft of chapter 1. It was like opening a door and stepping into a new world. I've learned so much from my writers' guild friends. I never would have put together the book I have without the support, advice, and edits from my friends there. Thank you very much especially to William, the Klamath Writers' Guild president; and Dotty, Jean, Bill, Ed, Ken, Kate, and Maggie who spent days reviewing and editing my manuscripts. I never would have pulled it all together without you.

Thank you also to Matt, my husband, and Judy, my mom, who read and reread my manuscripts many times.

Thanks to Laura, a friend, who put words from tape onto CDs for me.

Thanks to my best friend, Deena, and my stepmother, Catherine, who also read my manuscripts and kept encouraging me to keep writing even when I felt like giving up.

There are so many people out there that supported me during the three years it took me to pull this book together. I hope you all know how much I appreciate it.

Thank you to my two boys, Grant and Clint, who inspired me to stay alive and keep going.

Most of all, thank you to my Lord Jesus. I am an empty shell without him.

PROLOGUE

Pitch-black. I only saw snow and ice a short distance ahead in the light of my headlamp. Fingers ached, stiff in my gloves. Toes numb in my mountaineering boots. I climbed up the steep slope of California's Mount Shasta in the freezing night air. Kicking my crampons into the rock-hard ice kept me from sliding dangerously down the mountain. I carried an ax in one hand, ready to slam it into the ice to stop myself if I fell. My goal was to make it to the peak, 14,167-foot elevation.

It wasn't the first mountain I'd climbed in my life. From a hard childhood to adult years, I'd climbed many life's mountains as most people do.

When I was seven years old, my family of five crumbled. My parents divorced, and quickly, the family I loved began to disappear, one by one.

Cheryl's family before divorce

First, my dad was gone; he moved to a different home. Then within a year, my older brother, Willy, faded away. After the divorce, he began hitting me often, so Mom sent him off to live with Dad, not knowing what else to do to protect me. Then my little brother, Scott, started getting into trouble at school; soon after that, he vanished too. Mom sent him off to live with Dad. My family went from five to two. Life felt empty and filled with holes.

Mom worked as a loan officer at a bank in town and didn't get home until dinnertime. After school, each day, I rushed home. After locking the front door, I sat in a rocking chair, looking out the window, and waited. The living room didn't feel alive; it was silent and hollow. I was all alone.

During the summer school breaks, Mom dropped me off at Dad's house, next to Grandma and Grandpa's on the family prune farm. I loved being reconnected with my brothers, but time spent with Dad was often scary to me. Since we were little, Dad always practiced old-time discipline he learned from his German father, whipping us if we didn't meet his expectations. He'd smack us, not only with his hand, but with a belt, a stick, or something else in reach.

My brothers and I drove tractors during prune harvest when we were old enough, around ten. Our job was loading empty bins onto the harvester and bins full of prunes onto the flatbed semi-truck. Once we didn't work fast enough, and Dad broke a stick off a nearby prune tree and smacked us.

I learned to never cry when disciplined. If Dad heard us cry during a spanking, he would whip us more and say, "I'll give you something to cry about!" I remember once getting welts on my lower back from his belt. Taking a bath that evening, it stung so badly I could barely lower myself into the warm water. But I held the tears in and didn't cry.

Not long after my parents divorced, Dad started seeing a new woman. Her hair, bright as fire, she was known as Red. We didn't get along; tension was high. She joined my dad in discipline, usually using her favorite weapon—a wooden spoon.

Cheryl driving tractor during prune harvest

It seemed easy to set her off. Once I wasn't washing the dishes quite right and got a whack with the spoon on the side of my head.

During my sixth-grade school year, I went to a week long vacation Bible school at a church two blocks from where Mom and I lived. A few days later, a man named Pat showed up at our doorstep. He informed my mom about the church and invited us to attend. We began going to service each Sunday, and seven months later, Pat and my mom were married.

We moved into his home, with him and his three children: Liesl, Jenny, and Jimmy. I quickly went from being an only child to being surrounded by many siblings. Liesl and I were the same age, and Jenny and Jimmy were one and two years younger. Soon Mom brought Scott, the same age as Jimmy, back to live with us. Willy visited off and on, but wanted to stay living with Dad.

Six kids – Cheryl, Liesl, Willy, Jimmy, Scott, Jenny

The change started out hard. Liesl and Jenny could be cruel with words, making me feel I didn't belong. But soon we started watching *The Brady Bunch* on TV in the evenings together. We laughed, feeling we were the true Brady Bunch, and began enjoying our new large family. Mom quit her job to stay at home with all of us kids. I was so happy she was there every day when I walked in the door after school.

During my teenage years, I climbed more life mountains as most teens do. After high school, I went to Humboldt State University and studied to be a wildlife biologist. There I met a wonderful guy, Matt, another wildlife student. We spent time walking along the ocean beach, bird-watching and studying together. We fell in love. One day, after I graduated, we got married and built dreams for our future.

Cheryl and Matt's Wedding

Ten years later, in June of 2000, our life had been blessed. Matt and I owned a great home, we had two amazing sons—Grant and Clint—and we both had great jobs as wildlife biologists. We were satisfied and happy.

Then the largest, most overwhelming, life's mountain I'd ever climbed loomed before me. I was diagnosed with cancer; grade 4 Glioblastoma Multiforme, the most deadly brain tumor.

I was told I had less than a year to live.

CHAPTER 1

How the Climb Began

It began one spring morning. The sun was out and the weather crisp. I stood in a chicken coop adjacent to the barn. A high chain-link fence kept raccoons and skunks from stealing poultry at night. Cool air held down the stink of chicken droppings that always stuck to the bottom of my shoes.

Matt and I had purchased and settled in on thirty-two acres, located in the transition zone between the Rogue Valley and the mixed coniferous forestlands of southwestern Oregon. A home, painted bluish-gray with a metal roof to match, was situated to the edge of the property near the county road. The original foundation, built in the early 1900s, had round timbers that supported the walls and floor structure. Behind the home sat the barn.

The property was on a hillside covered with mixed Douglas fir, madrone, and white oak trees. Spring rain had greened up the leaves and needles. Yellow tulips and blue crocus sprouts had already broken through the soil and were beginning to flower.

In beat-up old clothes and black rubber boots, I held a sharp machete in one hand and a chicken in the other. Thirty hens shuffled around me. I took a deep breath, not looking forward to the butchering day. Even though our family loved to eat homegrown broilers, killing them was not fun.

Watching me closely out of the corner of their eyes, they scratched the ground, appearing to know they would soon become BBQ dinner. I stared back at them, trying to avoid eye contact. To get the work done, I headed toward the chopping block. Matt, being a helpful husband, created a butcher table for me by laying a piece of plywood on two sawhorses. It was slightly off balance and wobbly. I hoped it wouldn't tip over. Chickens started clucking.

Grant and Clint's laughs reverberated in the distance through the open window of our home. Most likely they were wrestling with

Daddy. Grant, three years old, had enough energy to power the universe. With black hair, dark eyes, and dimpled cheeks, he always ran around with confidence. He loved to wrestle with Daddy. Clint, one year old, liked to cuddle more than wrestle. With large round greenish eyes, he was good at getting what he wanted with his big puppy stare. It was hard to say no to him.

I pouted and thought, *I'd rather be in the house with Matt and the boys.* But butchering was my task, since I was the one who wanted to raise the poultry in the first place: eight egg-laying hens, two roosters, two turkeys, and thirty meat chickens.

I loved the farmyard atmosphere, providing our family with our own meat. Matt had already hunted and dressed out a deer, elk, and turkey that year. We planned to fill up our large freezer full of wild and homegrown meat. It was my turn to add to it.

To encourage myself, I said out loud, "You guys are going to be tasty!" Laying a chicken on the block, I stuck its head between two nails, pulled on its legs to stretch the neck out, then swung the machete. Off came the head; out shot the blood.

At that exact moment, I felt a sharp pain slam into my left temple. Like a jab from an ice pick. Dropping the headless body, I bent over in pain. The nearby chickens stopped clucking and watched. In silence, I could only hear my heart pulsating in my left ear. *Had the chickens cursed me? What was happening?* Sinking to the ground, I held my head between my hands, chicken blood smearing across my cheeks.

After a few moments, I took a deep breath and grabbed the plywood to pull myself up. The chickens began clucking and scratching the ground again. I closed my eyes tightly for a few seconds then opened them again and looked around. My sight was normal. Raised by my Dad to believe work before pleasure, I thought to myself. *Keep working and get it done.*

Chicken after chicken, I grabbed the nearest, sat it on the butcher block, and chopped. Then I tightly held each one neck down in a garbage can until the wings stopped flapping and the blood stopped draining. With a sharp knife, I sliced open the skin, cut off the breasts and legs. I felt the warm smooth muscles in the fresh meat. The scent of blood was like a paved road on a hot day.

Cheryl butchering chickens

Matt, Clint, and Grant on the Griffin Lane property

Thirty chickens later, I put all the meat in a big plastic container and headed to the house to clean and wrap it for the freezer.

I walked in the back door, arms full of chicken meat. Matt came into the kitchen and asked, "Do you want some help finishing it off?"

"Yes, thanks. I've got the worst headache. I feel like my own head got chopped. Let's hurry and get this done so I can lie down." When we finished the job, I washed the blood away, took some Tylenol, stripped my clothes off, and crawled into bed.

The headache went on for weeks with peaks and valleys of intensity, but always there. The pressure pounded. It even hurt to bend over and tie my shoes. With each step, it felt like my skull would explode. Despite the excruciating pain, I continued to go to work each day as well as take care of things at home. Telling myself, *Tough it out.*

One afternoon, Matt, the boys, and I took our pony, Butterfinger, out for a ride. I don't know how he ever got that name because he sure wasn't sweet like the candy bar. He quickly tried to get you off his back any way he could. He at least deserved credit for creativity.

When it was my turn to ride the pony, we headed down a road on a fairly steep slope. Matt carried Clint in a backpack, and Grant walked alongside him. Butterfinger stopped quickly and lowered his head and shoulders as if he wanted to take a bite of grass that didn't even exist on the road. He flung me forward over his shoulders, and I hit the ground headfirst. Slowly I sat up, my hair tangled with leaves, sticks, and dirt. I didn't care.

Matt ran forward and grabbed me. "Are you OK?"

"Please take him. I have to go," I whined, holding my head. Matt grabbed the pony by the reins and followed me home, with Grant running alongside.

That night I couldn't sleep; the pressure in my head was unbearable. "You need to go to the emergency room!" Matt exclaimed. "I'll take you."

Grant, Matt, Clint and Cheryl with Butterfinger

"No, I can drive myself," I said. "You stay home with the boys. I don't want to call somebody in the middle of the night and ask them to baby-sit."

I rushed to the emergency room and described the pain to the doctor. The first thing he said was, "It's just a normal headache."

"What? No, it's not!" I argued and pointed to my left temple. "I can feel something in there. If I shake my head, it moves."

He looked at me like I made it up. "Why don't you go home, take some Tylenol, and relax. It will go away."

Earlier that evening, I had gotten on the Internet and Googled "headache." One Web page described five symptoms that raised red flags. If you met three, it was not a normal headache. I had all five.

I told the doctor, "I want a CAT scan. This isn't normal."

He gave me a stupid smile again and told me to come back in a few weeks if it hadn't gone away. Angrily, I stomped out the door. If I hadn't been in such pain, I would have argued with him more. I was in no mood for a fight.

Two days later, we flew east to visit Matt's family in New Hampshire and Massachusetts, where he grew up. We'd purchased the plane tickets months before and didn't want to waste them. We wanted Grant and Clint to have the opportunity to visit with their faraway East Coast family that they rarely saw. I figured a relaxing vacation might be the exact thing I needed to get rid of my headache.

During our trip, we stayed at Matt's mom's home (Catherine, "Grammy Cat") and were busy visiting Matt's dad (Grandpa Joe); the boy's great-grandparents (Gummy and Gumpy and Grandpa Broyles); and Matt's cousins, aunts, and uncles. My headache got worse and worse. I often sneaked off by myself to hide in a quiet room. All the busy noises and movements were too much for my brain to handle. Catherine gave me a full bottle of aspirin, but no matter how many tablets I took, it didn't phase my headache.

Early one morning, it got to the point where I was in so much pain I couldn't open my eyes. I shook Matt, woke him up, and said, "We've got to go, we've got to go."

Matt quickly woke his mom and told her, "We need to go to the emergency room. Can I borrow your car? Please watch the boys for us."

Catherine, shocked and scared, said, "Yes, yes, go."

Matt helped me to the car and drove as fast as he safely could, not worrying about getting a speeding ticket. My brain couldn't think clearly, and everything went black. All I could do was hold my head and rock back and forth, crying.

At the ER exam room, the nurse asked me questions, "Describe the pain. How would you rank it, from one to ten?" The pain was so intense I couldn't speak, just continued rocking back and forth. Without delay, she injected my arm with medication. I felt it slowly crept into my veins and through my body, like sinking into a nice warm bath. Finally, I could take a deep breath, relax, and open my eyes. The pain went completely away.

"Thank you," was all I said. I felt so relieved.

Lying on a gurney, I was rolled off to get a CT scan. After the scan, Matt and I waited in a hospital room for results. Once I began to think more clearly, fear rushed in. Fear replaced the pain; it wasn't any better. On the phone near the hospital bed, Matt called our family members to update them on what was happening. Hearing him describe it all, made it seem so real. Nausea and cramps from fear hit my stomach. I ran to the nearest bathroom, where stuff came rushing out of both ends. Thank goodness the sink sat adjacent to the toilet.

The doctor returned, placing the scanned film in the x-ray viewer on the wall. Looking to me in the eyes, with a solid unemotional expression, he said, "Your brain is hemorrhaging in the left temporal lobe. We're going to send you by ambulance to a larger hospital to see a specialist."

I couldn't respond. I could only stare at my brain scan. The next thing I knew, I was rushed off to the UMass Memorial Medical Center, forty-five minutes away. Matt followed, keeping up with the ambulance in his mom's car. There were no lights or sirens on, but the ambulance exceeded the speed limit and moved right along. I can't remember much of the trip other than the fear and the pressure of belts that held my chest, arms, and legs tight to the gurney. The paramedic sat quietly next to me, taking my vital signs over and over again.

At the hospital, they took me straight in for an MRI. Pushed from one room to another, here to there, it all happened so quickly. Soon after, a doctor with a caring smile and sweet eyes leaned over me; putting his hand on my shoulder, he said, "You needed to have brain surgery to stop the hemorrhaging."

All I thought to say was, "Can I fly home to Oregon for surgery?" I didn't want to be over two thousand miles away from home with a risk of coming out of a craniotomy with serious disabilities.

"Yes," was all I remember him saying.

Checked out of the hospital, Matt and I headed back to Grammy Cat's house. We needed to find a neurosurgeon in Oregon ASAP. Grammy Cat, knowing we were so focused on finding a surgeon, was so helpful and took the boys out to play at a park, fed them, gave them baths, and put them to bed for us.

Sitting at her kitchen table, we spent hours on the phone. I wasn't sure the little town of Medford had a brain surgeon. We also weren't quite sure how to find one in Oregon from across the country. In the past, I'd searched telephone books for hair salons and car mechanics, but never for a neurosurgeon. Directory assistance gave me one Medford number to try.

I called and a woman receptionist answered the phone. "I'm looking for a neurosurgeon with craniotomies experience," I said.

I'd been told most neurosurgeons have practice with operating on spines and other things like carpal tunnel syndrome, but not on brains.

"Yes, Dr. so-and-so does craniotomies," she said confidently.

To make sure the doctor was well qualified, I asked, "How many brain surgeries has he done?"

"One," she said. I hung up the phone. I wanted to find a specialized neurosurgeon, one that did brain surgery every day, all year long. One that could do it with his eyes closed. That's what I wanted. Later I found out the receptionist was probably being sarcastic, but how was I to know.

Matt called a coworker at the BLM, who'd gone through brain surgery a few years before. He recommended that we use his neurosurgeon at the Oregon Health & Science University (OHSU) in Portland, only a five-hour drive north of home. We quickly called OHSU and scheduled an appointment for surgery.

The next day we flew to Portland. I carried a big manila envelope with the MRI films with me. Matt and I could tell Grant and Clint sensed something was up. We looked worried. The boys looked anxious and confused. Still in shock, we didn't know what to tell them. So we tried to smile, gave them treats to eat, toys to play with, and held them close on the flight back to Oregon.

My brother Scott, who lived in Salem, an hour south of Portland, met us at the airport. "Grant and Clint, you get to have a sleepover at Uncle Scott and Aunt Sue's house," I told them as Uncle Scott reached down to give them each a hug, then pulled me tight into one. At first they hesitated, but their reaction changed quickly when I told them, "You get to play with Emily and Zack." Loving their cousins, they jumped at that idea.

After Matt and I gave the boys big hugs, they climbed into Uncle Scott's car. My brother held me tight, and I could tell by the look in his eyes, he didn't really know what to say. "Thank you, Scott," I said and waved good-bye as they drove off.

Will this be the last time I see my boys?

Grant and Clint

CHAPTER 2

CHECKING IN FOR BRAIN SURGERY

After I checked in to Oregon Health & Science University (OHSU), a nurse led me to an assigned room and gave me an armload of clean, but well-used patient clothes. Dr. Delashaw, the neurosurgeon, agreed to work me into his busy schedule, but was still trying to figure out how. Consequently, I was put on "hold." On the phone, I'd been on hold many times in the past and had grown to hate it. I figured being on hold in the hospital would be even worse.

I was right.

During that time I wasn't allowed to eat. My stomach needed to be empty when the anesthesiologist put me under surgery so I wouldn't vomit and choke. An IV fed me glucose and water to prevent dehydration. However, it didn't cut back the stomach aching and grumbling hungry feeling. That feeling brought out the worst in me, an attitude of anger. On "hold" for three days without food, my bad mood bubbled. I could lose it and yell at anyone and everyone, but Matt got most of it.

"Don't you eat that in front of me!" I yelled if Matt walked in the hospital room with food. If he tried to show me empathy, I'd yell, "Don't touch me! Don't you understand? I'm starving!" Anything set me off, even if Matt moved wrong. I had to bite my tongue with the nurse. I knew Matt loved me and would forgive, but not the nurse. I needed to be nice to her so she wouldn't gouge me with a needle when she removed what seemed like a gallon of blood for tests each day.

During the wait, the doctor ordered an angiogram to figure out what caused the hemorrhaging in my brain. With the pocket of blood surrounding and hiding the area of interest, an MRI couldn't show the details clearly. An anesthesiologist injected me with drugs so I would be awake, but relaxed and feeling no pain during the angiogram. A doctor cut a slice in my groin area and slid a very small snakelike tube up through a blood vessel, past my heart and into my brain. I lay there and watched a TV-like screen as the tube slowly crept its way through the vessels in my brain. It looked like a train traveling through underground tunnels to me. I wondered what the doctor saw, but was too overwhelmed to ask.

After the angiogram, Dr. Delashaw told me that an abnormal mass of arteries and veins called an arteriovenous malformation (AVM) caused the hemorrhage. The arteries and veins were slowly leaking blood. As the blood leaked out, it raised the pressure inside my skull, squeezing my brain and causing my headache. As he described it, I envisioned a balled-up clump of noodles covered with red spaghetti sauce. Removing the misplaced dinner sounded reasonable to me. I wanted it out fast.

During my long wait for surgery, family and friends surrounded me with love. Thank goodness I had a phone on the table next to my bed because I got call after call, even from people I hadn't talked with in years. The nearby table was also covered with vases of flowers. One afternoon, a friend from back home in Medford showed up with her three elementary-aged children, and they all prayed for me. With all the attention from family and friends, I had never before felt so loved and supported. It amazed me.

Finally, when I felt like I'd starved to death, a nurse walked in and said, "You're going into surgery now;" then gave me an injection. She explained that Dr. Delashaw planned to do the surgery concurrently on me and another woman, walking back and forth between the two operating rooms.

I was so nervous when the nurse rolled me away, I don't remember saying good-bye to Matt. I just remember him walking alongside my gurney, holding my hand until the nurse brought me into a pre-surgery room and left me lying there alone. Everything there looked pure white and clean. The bright lights above me were blinding. The room seemed empty, other than me lying in the center of it.

Soon, in walked two anesthesiologists. One looked like Catwoman; and the other, with a thick German accent, sounded like

Adolph Hitler when he said hello. Then looking down at his records, he said, "Cheryl, we're your anesthesiologists today during surgery." The nurse must have injected me with some serious drugs because I actually began to laugh and panic at the same time.

My mind shifted to the Holocaust.

Matt and I had recently spent time in Washington, DC. It was a special trip for me to receive a national award. The American Forest & Paper Association presented me a Wildlife Stewardship Award for improving and protecting wildlife habitat on private forestlands. It was a significant and exciting event for me as a wildlife biologist from a small town in Oregon. During the dinner, when I received the award up on the stage, Matt stood and clapped with a proud smile on his face. It meant a lot to me that he was there.

While in DC, I wanted to spend a day at the Holocaust Museum. Matt had other museums he wanted to see. We decided to head out in separate directions that morning and meet back up that afternoon.

My grandpa Gard had fought in World War II. Shot down in his P-38 fighter plane, he'd been held as a prisoner of war for over a year by the Germans. I felt connected to that time and always wanted to learn more about it. In school, I'd been taught about the general history, but never exposed to the details of the cruel, horrible life Jewish, elderly, and disabled people suffered during Hitler's reign.

Checking into the museum, I was given an ID card/brochure containing the identity and description of a woman who suffered in the Holocaust. Walking into each different section of the museum, I would stop and read more about what happened to her personally. I could barely breathe; it felt like I was living the life along with her. Toward the end of my museum tour, she was killed in a gas chamber. It felt like part of me died with her. I was in gloom the rest of the day.

The day of surgery, I was still under the effects of the Holocaust Museum. The drugs the anesthesiologist gave me, my Holocaust thoughts, and the German accent were a bad combination. So when Hitler leaned over my bed and began talking to me, I thought I was doomed to be put to sleep for good. I started to shake and thought I would shimmy right off the side of the bed and slam onto the hard cold floor.

Catwoman leaned over me from the other side and held me gently. She must have been concerned I'd shimmy off the bed too. I turned to look at her and saw her red curly hair sticking out in all directions. Her eyeglasses convinced me she was Catwoman. The narrow frames curved up at the outer edge like cat eyes. I tried to hold in a nervous laugh. *Catwoman is a good hero, right? She'll protect me from the doom of Hitler, won't she?*

They pumped me up with more drugs and rolled me into the operating room. More bright lights aimed down at me. People dressed in white hurried around the room setting up things for surgery. They never paused and looked at me or stopped by my side to say hello. I was just another patient. At least they had some good old rock-and-roll music playing in the background. I closed my eyes and tried to relax.

I took a deep breath, opened my eyes, and rolled my head to the side, getting a good view of the MRI brain scan hanging up on the wall. *That's not my brain! It's someone else's!* The abnormal "spot" was located on the wrong side of the brain and looked twice as big as mine. I started to panic.

I'd read horrible stories about doctors making surgery mistakes, and the worry about it hit me. Oh no, do they think that's me? What if they cut into the wrong side of my brain? Would I end up with brain missing from both sides? I'll end up a vegetable! My heart started pounding, and my chest tightened. But I didn't want to point out the wrong MRI to someone and offend them. Just like never wanting to offend a waiter in a restaurant for fear they might spit in your food. I didn't want to anger anybody in the operating room and motivate them to spit into my brain full of AVM spaghetti noodles.

Catwoman, my hero, obviously noticed my skyrocketing blood pressure and heart rate. She leaned over me, smiling, and messed around with the IV in my arm. Off to sleep I went. As it turned out, the MRI film was of the previous patient that day and just hadn't been replaced with mine yet.

CHAPTER 3

DIAGNOSIS

In what seemed like seconds, I woke up. My shoulder shook, and someone said "Open your eyes." I tried to peel them open; they didn't cooperate. My mind walked through a deep fog, unable to find its way out. It wanted to hibernate. Through the slits of my eyelids, I saw an obscure movement above me that said, "What is your name?"

Must be a nurse. I ignored her, thinking she should already know my name. My eyes and mouth wouldn't open anyway. She kept shaking me. "What is you name? What is the date and time?"

After a while, annoyed and wanting her to leave me alone, I whispered, "Cheryl." She seemed happy with that and left. Again I went off to sleep, hibernating in a cave with a black bear.

The first night and day after surgery, I slept off and on in a daze. If awake, I'd reach and feel the side of my head. There was no mirror, so I couldn't see myself. My fingers moved softly around the wound, gently crawling over the stitches like a spider. I tried to visualize what it looked like. Dr. Delashaw had shaved a medium-sized circle area above my left ear. The remaining hair around it was covered with gooey chunks of drying blood and Vaseline-like gel they'd used to hold my hair back from the hole they cut in my head.

Matt was allowed in the recovery room with me. He sat by my side, held my hand, and assured me he'd called and updated family. At night he slept in a chair beside the bed. Every hour a nurse came in and took my vital signs. I would look over and see Matt beside me. Comforted, I'd fall back asleep. After the first twenty-four hours, Matt finally left my side and went south to my brother's house to take a shower and check on Grant and Clint.

When I was fully alert, a nurse moved me to the neuro ward. Once settled in, I noticed the other woman in the bed next to mine. The bandages on her head told me she'd also been through brain surgery. She couldn't move her body, except one hand, a little bit. The nurse had placed a button in that hand to push if she needed help. Generally she lay still and very quiet. When her parents visited, she rarely talked. When she did, it came out as a forced whisper.

A nurse told me that my roommate, Kate, was the person Dr. Delashaw did surgery on concurrently with me. She and I were often alone in the room. I wanted to approach her and introduce myself, but I didn't know how. I didn't know if she wanted to meet a stranger, especially since talking was a struggle for her.

She often hit the nurse button without getting any response. I got up and went to her side to see if I could help. She smiled. "Yes, the water." I held her cup to her mouth, and she sipped water from the straw.

"Your first?" Kate asked.

Knowing exactly what she meant, "Yes."

"My ninth . . . in the base," she said with a smile.

I sat down on the chair next to her, and our friendship began. Over the next two days, most of my time was at her bedside. We spent hours in deep conversation—topics no one else would ever talk about unless they'd gone through brain surgery. My side of the conversation was fairly normal, but Kate spoke only in short slow sentences.

I helped her all I could. I got her sips of water, repositioned her on the bed when her hip began to hurt, and tracked down the nurse when she needed more pain medication. But in the end, she helped me more than I helped her. She had so much to share with me, and she had such a hard time speaking. I felt blessed that she would go through such an effort to encourage me.

In seven years, she'd gone through nine brain surgeries. The tumor, considered benign, was located in her brain stem at the base of her skull. The brain stem controls subconscious functions, like breathing and heart beating. Each time the tumor grew back, she needed surgery to save her life. After each surgery, Kate came out more and more disabled. After number 9, she couldn't walk. Amazed by her facial expression filled with love and peace, I couldn't help asking, "After all you've been through and now being mostly paralyzed, is it still worth living?"

She looked at me, her eyes glowing with wisdom, and said slowly, with honesty, "Yes, I appreciate every second. They are blessings from God. It is worth living as long as I can." I held her hand and we cried together.

When not at Kate's side, I walked loops around the neuro ward hallways. The hallway was quiet, no one else moving around except, occasionally, a nurse walking by. A bag filled with liquid medication was attached to an IV in my arm. The bag hung on what I called "the stick on wheels." I pulled it alongside me, swerving around obstacles in the hallway; a bed to my left, a machine to my right. I speed-walked as fast as I could, careful not to hook the IV tube on something, ripping the needle from my arm.

In the neuro ward, all the other patients had gone through brain surgery too. Out of curiosity, I slowed down at each door and peeked into the room. All the people were older than me. Kate and I were both in our early thirties. The others seemed sixty or older. Each of them lay still and quiet in bed. *Are they completely incapable? Will that be me one day?* My recovery seemed so different than Kate's and all the others' in the neuro ward. *I don't belong here!* My eyes searched for a quick way to sneak out a back door. I didn't see an EXIT door on the third floor, so I ended up back in bed.

After a day or two of this, when my doctor walked in my room, the first thing I asked was, "Can I check out of this place?"

He smiled. "You look good. We'll talk about it. Let me take a look." Dr. Delashaw walked over and checked out my stitches.

Matt, sitting next to me, asked, "What did you find during surgery?"

My doctor looked at Matt, then at me. "Hidden within the AVM we found a tumor, the size of an acorn."

A long pause as he watched for my reaction. Matt and I just stared at him, waiting for his next words. "It looks like you can check out tomorrow. Come back in two weeks for a checkup. At that point, we'll have results from the pathology test, and we'll know if the tumor was malignant or not."

"OK," I said. Reaching for Matt's hand, I rolled over and tried to force myself to sleep, wanting to hide from the reality of what I'd just been told.

The next morning, a nurse pushed me in a wheelchair to the exit door. Matt walked silently beside me. I finally asked her a question, even though I knew neither of us would like the answer. "How does brain cancer actually kill someone? What actually happens?" I knew how lung, breast, and colon cancer got you; but brain cancer was a mystery to me.

The wheelchair stopped abruptly. The nurse looked right at me and said, "There's limited room within a skull. When the tumor grows, it takes over the space. With no place to go, the brain is squished and not able to survive." She said it casually as if describing how to make a peanut-butter-and-jelly sandwich. I swallowed back the bile that worked its way up my throat. If my brain didn't survive, the rest of me wouldn't either. I stood up and walked slowly out of the hospital. I never wanted to go back to that place. But that wasn't an option.

On the five-hour drive home to Medford, I asked Matt to keep the radio off. I needed silence. Any stimulation overwhelmed me. Bright shapes and sounds flashed by as we drove down the highway. My brain wanted to hide. I pulled a loose-fitting hat over my eyes and covered my ears with my hands. I wanted to curl up in a fetal position in a dark, quiet room. I could tell my brain was shutting down like a computer infected with a virus. *Things will never be the same again.* I never considered myself beautiful or outgoing. The only thing I was proud about myself was my quick brain: great at organizing, multitasking, and problem solving. *Why, of all things, brain cancer? Why didn't I get breast cancer? I'd rather lose a breast or an arm or leg. Not my cognitive abilities. What will be left of me if I can't think?*

My brain was worn-out and fatigued. It seemed to be moving slowly, disabled. *What will happen when I get home? I can't keep up with Grant and Clint, so loud and energetic.* Grant liked to wrestle and take hikes in our forest. He loved for Mommy to read him books. Clint wanted me to carry him everywhere. At his age, he wanted me to do everything with him—eating, bathing, sleeping, and playing—as if I was an extension of his body. *Can I be the mommy my boys want and need?* Matt drove quietly beside me. *Will I ever again be the wife he married? Will we ever retire together one day and grow old together?* As wildlife biologists, we had dreams of retiring one day and traveling the world, volunteering with the Peace Corps, working with marsupial animals in Australia and New Zealand.

I turned my face away from Matt, not wanting him to see me cry.

When we pulled into our driveway, I took a deep breath, happy to remember my mom had picked up Grant and Clint from my brother's house and brought them home to our place. She was going to stay for a week to help take care of me and them. Mom always spoiled me. Matt also planned to stay home for a week. I smiled.

I walked into the house, gave my boys and my mom (Mema to the boys) big hugs, and crawled into bed. The boys, usually so energetic and rowdy, seemed to know things were different. Their quietness was exactly what I needed. I fell asleep, comforted, knowing that Mema would read the boys a story when she tucked them into bed. Mema would give them lots of love.

Grant and Clint

During my recovery time, Grant and Clint were so sweet. They often crawled quietly into bed and cuddled with me. Their soft warm skin pressed against mine; their warm breath moved across my neck. Their energy was like magic, entering and healing me. I held them tight; I knew I had to get better.

Two weeks after the craniotomy, Matt and I went back to Portland to see Dr. Delashaw. He said, "The pathology results confirm the tumor was malignant, an anaplastic oligodendroglioma. I'll refer you to our neuro-oncologist to arrange for chemotherapy and radiation." I stared out the window, my mind wandering off into space. Again, I wanted to hide. Matt did most of the talking. I do remember Dr. Delashaw saying, "When you get home, don't spend hours on the Internet reading everything about brain tumors. It will discourage you. Don't pay attention to statistics. You're not a number, you're an individual." Later, I realized it was one of the nicest and most valuable things he could have said to me.

The neuro-oncologist told Matt and I about all the standard treatments available for malignant brain tumors. He encouraged me to be part of a chemotherapy clinical trial, "Every two weeks, a catheter would be fed up through the blood vessels in your groin into your brain, and chemotherapy drugs would be injected directly into your tumor cavity." Since it was an experiment, it was still unclear how the tumor or body would respond. There was a risk that the treatment itself would kill me; I would be the guinea pig. I left Portland feeling emotionally paralyzed. I didn't like the high risk; I wanted a second opinion.

Matt and I decided to consult the University of California San Francisco (UCSF), a hospital with a specialized Department of Neurosurgery/Oncology. OHSU sent my medical records and a pathology slice of the tumor down to UCSF. A week later, Matt and I sat in the San Francisco neuro-oncologist's office; and he went over all the options I could choose from, as if it were a menu from a high-class restaurant. I wished it were that easy. Nothing on his list sounded palatable either. I took my "menu" and stood to leave, and he said, "I'll call you in a few days with the pathologist's results. We can then finalize what treatments you'll take."

I left San Francisco hoping the second pathology opinion would determine the tumor was benign.

CHAPTER 4

WHY ME?

The first month after surgery, July 2000, I ignored Dr. Delashaws's advice and spent hours on the Internet researching brain tumors. I bought every book I could find on fighting cancer.

I learned that glioma tumors were graded, I through IV. The anaplastic oligodendroglioma I was diagnosed with was grade 1. The worst of the worst, the glioblastoma multiforme (GBM), was grade 4. Unlike lower-grade gliomas, GBMs spread into the brain like tentacles and quickly take over and kill the brain tissue around them. According to statistics at that time, GBMs killed patients within months of diagnosis; 95 percent of them died within a year. The prognosis was considered "terminal."

Grant, Clint, and I were playing with LEGOS, building monsters, when the phone rang. "Hold on, boys," I said, running over to pick it up.

I will never forget that moment.

"Pathologist's results show you have a glioblastoma multiforme. We sent the tumor to Johns Hopkins for a third opinion, and they agreed. It's not an anaplastic oligodendroglioma, but a GBM. You need to come back here right away."

I hung up the phone and dropped to the floor. I felt like throwing up. My heart pounded; my chest hurt. My eyes swelled with tears. *How long will I live? Will I hear Clint say his first sentence? Will I see Grant start kindergarten? If I died within a year, would they even remember me? Would I leave Matt alone, a single dad?*

Grant and Clint saw me on the floor hyperventilating. They rushed over and touched me. They were scared. "Mommy, Mommy, are you OK?" Grant asked.

They shouldn't see me this way. I need to get away.

"I'm OK. Do you want to watch *Barney*?" I asked. They smiled, and I popped in a *Barney* video. The purple dinosaur danced around.

I called Matt, "You have to come home. You need to watch the boys. UCSF says I have a GBM."

Matt knew what I did about the different brain tumor grades. He knew it was bad news. "I'll be there as fast as I can."

Matt had been dispatched to fight forest fires in southwestern Oregon. He'd just spent the day leading a crew of twenty firefighters, digging line on the Antioch Road fire. When I called, he'd just returned to the BLM office. Before heading home, he had to take time to work with the dispatch center to find a replacement to lead the crew the next day.

Thirty minutes later, he pulled into the driveway. He walked in the door as I walked out saying, "I need some time. We can talk about it later, OK?"

"I would have been home sooner, but needed to find a replacement. Take the time you need. I'll be here." Matt gave me a hug, held me tight, and then went inside with the boys.

I headed for my favorite spot in the forest, uphill from our home. It was a small shady area under a low-crowned Douglas fir. From there, I could look out and see a view of the Rogue Valley. What I liked best was leaning up against the tree's bark, feeling its texture. The smell of the soil, cones, and needles calmed me.

I always felt at peace in the woods and needed it more than ever. I got to my spot and dropped to my knees, leaning over and digging my fingers into the soil. Crying out loud, I let it all out and didn't try to hide it. A puddle formed on the ground around me, merging tears, saliva, and phlegm that dripped from my eyes, nose, and mouth. My face muscles tightened and contorted until my cheeks and forehead ached.

I jumped up and raised my arms to God. "Why this! Why me!" I yelled. I had accepted Christ as my savior and followed God since I was a little girl. I'd been taught in the Bible that God expects us to learn and mature when we live through trials in our lives. So I asked, "What's this all about? What am I supposed to learn?" I listened and heard nothing. Frustrated, I yelled, "Why can't you tell me! Why do I need to go through cancer!" It felt like God had left me. There was nothing, but quietness.

I felt I was being tested, like Job in the Old Testament, to see if a trial could turn me against God. But I knew that would never happen. I would never lose my faith. So I looked up and defiantly yelled, "Fine, BRING IT ON!" I stopped and listened again. I still didn't hear anything. *I just challenged God! Was that a bad mistake? I'm stupid. God isn't going to talk to me.*

Suddenly, unexpectedly, I was covered with peace, like warm water running over me. My skin felt tingly, calm, and relaxed; a heavy weight was taken off my shoulders. My tears turned from pain to hope. I felt God there with me. He didn't have to say anything. I felt it. I wouldn't be alone. He would help me.

I stood up and walked slowly back to the house, wanting to be with Matt. *What's going to happen next?*

Matt and I settled in the corner of the living room holding each other tight while the boys continued watching TV. We talked softly so the boys couldn't hear us, and I told Matt about the pathologist's diagnosis. Then Matt, like me earlier, needed time alone. He got up and headed out to his favorite place, the workshop in the barn. I sat and watched the boys and thought about my time with them.

I'd worked for Boise Cascade Corporation for eight years, 7:00 AM to 5:00 PM, ten hours a day, five days a week. As a wildlife biologist, I worked with a team of foresters, engineers, and silviculturists. It was my job to protect wildlife habitat during timber harvest and other forest management. It was a challenge, but I loved it. I worked with threatened and endangered species like spotted owls and bald eagles and sensitive species like some salamanders, woodpeckers, and bats. My goal was to do everything I could to help protect the environment, the habitat, while the company harvested timber to turn a profit.

Cheryl and Matt with a Spotted owl

Grant, Cheryl, and Clint at the beach

WHY ME ?

When Grant and Clint were born, I wanted to quit my job to stay at home full-time with the boys, but I felt torn. Without my salary, we couldn't afford to live in our dream home, where Matt and I hoped to grow our own thirty-two acres of old-growth spotted owl habitat. If I quit my job, I'd also give up my influence on protecting wildlife habitat on the three hundred thousand acres in Western Oregon on Boise Cascade land. On top of that, I felt my mom and Pat's money spent on my college degree would be wasted.

With the diagnoses of terminal cancer, the important decision seemed easy to make. If I only have a year to live, I will spend every second I have with Grant and Clint. I will never go back to work again.

I knew that after the craniotomy, my brain was no longer capable of what it took to be a wildlife biologist. That challenge was beyond me. Playing with preschool-age kids was all I felt competent enough to do.

During a commercial on TV, the boys jumped up and ran over to crawl onto my lap. One on each leg, they gave me big hugs. Staying at home with the boys was the best decision I could make.

I'll do everything I can to keep cancer from ever taking me away from them

CHAPTER 5

A WATERFALL OF TEARS

People told me, "You're handing it all so well, it seems not to bother you at all." However, Matt and my friends who knew me well knew I was suffering and told me, "It's not healthy for you to hold it in. You have to cry and let it out."

In the back of my mind, I heard my dad's echo, "If you cry, I'll give you something to cry about!" So I had only allowed myself to sneak off, hide, and let the tears out a few times. There were still gallons trapped inside.

A friend of mine told me that some Native Americans believe tumors were formed from un-cried tears held inside. If Native American beliefs were true, I was surprised the neurosurgeon only found one brain tumor and not thousands in my head. I'd held in tears my whole life and a waterfall of them during the last few years before being diagnosed with cancer. I knew it was not healthy to hold them in and needed to do something to release them.

One afternoon, when Matt and the boys were busy playing together, I sneaked off by myself. My plan was to weep and cry and let it all out, to cleanse my spirit. But I still didn't want anyone to see. I walked up to my favorite part of our forest and settled down to start reliving my past.

During my early pregnancy with Clint, I had come down with chicken pox. Living through weeks with the virus was not too painful, but worrying about my unborn baby's health was. The doctor told me that having chicken pox during the early stage of pregnancy could cause deafness and loss of arms and legs in the infant. She ordered numerous ultrasounds to track the baby's development. I watched the screen as the wand moved over my

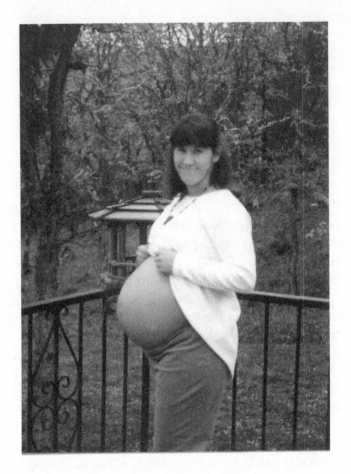

Cheryl pregnant with Clint

stomach. Worry tore at my heart. *Will the baby suffer? Is everything OK? It's my fault! It's my fault!*

I knew exactly where and when I got the virus. I'd volunteered in the day care room at church each Sunday for infants to two-year-old children. One morning, a youngster with chicken pox was brought in. The parents told me he was no longer contagious, even though his skin was still covered with little red spots. I played with the boy all morning. I didn't know that I'd never had chicken pox as a child. I didn't know it could cause damage to an unborn baby. *I should have known! I should have left the room!*

The doctor discussed the option of abortion, if the baby's defects were severe. Matt and I knew we loved our baby no matter what and decided abortion was not an option. During the stressful wait for the due date, more tears piled up inside. Months later, Clint was born healthy, but the hidden tears had taken their toll.

There had been other troubles during my pregnancy with Clint. Our well pump blew, and for over a week, we were without water. At that time, Matt was out of town elk hunting. He called me each evening to check up on me. One evening all he heard was, "Matt, come home now. The pump blew, and I have no water!"

It was a challenge for a pregnant lady to go without a toilet. Grant was two years old and, thank goodness, still in diapers! I had to hike up into the woods behind the house to go. While pregnant, that's about every thirty minutes! Going pee was not so hard, but number two was a trial! It was a challenge hanging on to a tree squatting, with my huge belly pushing between my knees, struggling not to fall over and roll down the hill. That event by itself may not seem like a big ordeal, but it was, any pregnant lady would agree. Pregnancy itself is a challenge: hormone changes, exhaustion, heartburn, and weight gain, on and on. Going to the bathroom outside, trying not to fall over, was the final straw. I lost it. But I didn't cry, even though I felt the pain building up inside (like constipation!).

When Matt arrived home, hard times continued. When the pump blew, oil from the electric motor leaked and covered the walls of the well with PCBs (polychlorinated biphenyl). PCBs are dangerous carcinogens. We were relieved when tests showed PCBs hadn't gotten into the holding tank or the pipes in our house, but it took thousands of dollars and many months to clean PCBs from the well.

Matt rented some fifty-five-gallon barrels and bought equipment to clean out the well. Every evening, after work, he spent hours soaping and scrubbing the casing of the well, then pumping the toxic water out through filters into the barrels. Considered hazardous waste, they were hauled off to a special dump. We hired professionals to test the water over and over as Matt continued to clean until it showed PCBs were gone and the water was pure. The cleaning process drained every penny from our savings and replaced it with anxiety. I should've cleaned out my hidden tears of high toxicity and let Matt haul them away to the dump too. But I held them inside, and they were building like water, ready to break through a dam.

Less than a year later, when Grant was two and Clint, six months old, more misery was added to the list. We lost four of our wonderful sled dogs. Our dogs were not just pets; they were part of our family.

During my college years with Nishka, my beautiful Alaskan malamute, I fell in love with sled dogs. I watched the Alaskan Iditarod race on TV and dreamed of having a sled dog team. Our first Christmas after college, Matt gave me the best present, a dogsled. I jumped up and hugged Matt. "Thank you, thank you, thank you!" At that time, it was what I hoped for. Matt and I sat by the Christmas tree, running our fingers through Nishka's fur and dreamed of our future sled dog team.

Soon we began getting more and more sled dogs. First we got Taiga, and when she was old enough, we had two dogs to sled with. But that was not fast enough for me. Next we added Shasta to the team; and when she was two, we bred her and kept three of her pups, Tok, Kobuk, and Kenai. By then, Nishka was getting old and needed to retire. To have an even team of six, we got another dog that was already trained, Susie.

Clinging to the sled behind six dogs racing through the snow was exhilarating. I only needed to yell, "Let's go!" And off they went. Yelping with excitement, they pulled hard, digging their claws and flinging snow up into my face. I had to wear sunglasses to see. I had to hold on as tight as possible because if I fell off, they would leave me behind. The dogs got fast enough that I entered Chemult's sled dog race with four of our dogs. The next winter, when I was pregnant with Clint, Matt raced with two dogs pulling him on cross-country skis.

Most of the time, I was the one who stood on the sled and raced the dogs. Matt was our equipment manager. Each time we ran the dogs he got all the gear together and loaded it in the truck. He upgraded the sled, making it faster, and built a better brake.

Matt on the dogsled with Nishka to the left

Our sled dogs: Suzie, Shasta, Taiga, Kobuk, Kenai, Tok

Matt even modified an adult tricycle bike so I could work out with the dogs during summertime. Later, when Grant was one, Matt strapped a car seat to the sled so Grant could race along with me. Grant always laughed and screamed with excitement. Both Grant and Clint loved to cuddle and play with the dogs. The malamutes' thick double-coated fur was incredibly velvety and full. The boys would bury their faces in the fur and run their fingers through its softness.

When our young male dogs, Tok and Kobuk, hit their maturity, they wanted to be dominant alpha males and killed our thirteen-year-old Nishka. At that age, he couldn't defend himself. While we were at work one day, they tore out his guts and ripped his throat. I asked Matt to bury him so I didn't have to look at him. Matt buried Nishka in the forest back behind our home, shedding many tears in the process.

The following week, Taiga, our alpha female, was killed, her throat torn. Shasta having three grown pups wanted to become the new alpha. She and Kenai, the female pup, killed Taiga. Again, I asked Matt to bury Taiga. He put her beside Nishka.

I was blown away. The dogs were our babies for years before Grant and Clint were born. They were loving and submissive to people, but aggressive and deadly with animals. The dogs had killed chickens, cats, and rabbits. Then they escalated to killing each other. When would it stop? I couldn't take the risk of them ever hurting a human, even though I could never see that happening.

We decided Kenai and Kobuk, the two most aggressive, had to be put down. Again, I asked Matt to take them to the vet to be euthanized. He held them tight as the veterinarian put them to sleep. When Matt came home, his eyes were red and swollen. He told me he thought he was weak, crying more than a woman. But he was the strong one. He let his tears out. I didn't even have the courage to be there at the vet office.

In just two weeks, we went from seven sled dogs to three. My dream of sledding was crushed. I often curled up in a ball and closed my eyes, rocking back and forth, but I didn't cry. Then I would get up and do yard work. Digging weeds helped me focus on finding the dandelions instead. I should have watered the garden with tears, but didn't. They stayed hidden deep inside.

Matt, Grant, Tulip and Storm

Not long after dealing with losing most of our dogs, Matt had to euthanize another pet, Storm, our pack goat. He was a large 150+ pound pure white goat with horns that curved beautifully up and over his head.

Matt and I loved to backpack, and when the boys were born, we were determined to continue. We got two large friendly pack goats, Storm and Tulip. We got them as babies and had fed them with milk bottles, so they grew up very friendly. We trained them to carry packs. When we went backpacking or out for a day hike, they carried our gear while Matt and I carried the boys. Storm had also carried out deer meat when Matt hunted. The goats followed us around like pet dogs. Storm loved to lean his weight on us so he would get scratched behind his ears.

One day, Storm began to grow a tumor on his side. It quickly got bigger and bigger, and he stopped eating. The veterinarian told us there was nothing he could do. The goat had cancer. It was hard seeing him standing with his head hanging low and his rib bones starting to stick out.

Matt walked Storm up the hill to the back of our forestland, tears falling as he walked. I watched them go, my heart breaking. I never saw Storm again. On a tree stump, Matt poured some grain, Storm's favorite snack. As Storm ate, he held a gun to Storm's head and pulled the trigger, then left his body there for nature to take care of. I could never walk into the woods where he lay. I hoped the coyotes, vultures, and bugs would hurry and do their job.

I sat under the Douglas fir tree and wept out all the tears I'd held in for years. The dam broke, and I didn't do anything to stop it. Tears rolled down my cheeks like a waterfall. I wept for worry and frustration and anger and loneliness and burdens too heavy to carry. I also sobbed for the miseries of my childhood—for being whipped, being left alone, being separated from my dad and brothers. And then I wept for cancer. I cried until my eyes went as dry as a desert.

I was exhausted. My eyes burned and my body ached. But I also felt a heavy weight had been lifted from my heart. I breathed deeply. A wave of calm flowed over me. A poison had been expelled. I felt blessed that I had learned to never hold it in again.

There will always be hard times in my life. A terminal cancer is the worst I've seen. In the future, I promise myself I will work my way through the trials and let my tears fall.

I went back to the house and picked up my Bible. I'd grown up with God's Word, but most of the time, it was hidden on a shelf. My heart told me to take it out and blow off the dust. Wisdom inside the Book would show me how to live my life through the hard times that bring tears. Words from a well-known hymn came to mind, and I had a new appreciation for it.

Amazing Grace how sweet the sound
That saved a wretch like me
I once was lost, but now I am found
Was blind, but now, I see
Through many dangers, toils and snares
I have already come
'Twas grace that brought me safe thus far
And grace will lead me home.
--John Newton 1779--

CHAPTER 6

NO TO CHEMO – YES TO HERBS

My neuro-oncologist pressed me to move ahead with chemotherapy and radiation. GBMs grow rapidly; there was no time to waste. The neurosurgeon had removed what he could see of the tumor; but GBM tentacles could still be embedded in my brain, like roots of a weed, ready to re-sprout and grow. I needed to follow the surgery with some treatment to deal with any cancer cells left in my brain.

Friends and family were very supportive in talking with me about my medical crisis. But when it came to helping me decide what treatment to take, no one wanted to speak up.

Not even Matt.

He didn't want to help choose which chemotherapy to torture me with, so he pulled away from helping with decision making. "Do what your heart tells you to do, what you believe in," was all he'd say.

Matt helped me every other way he could. He'd rub my back and hold me tight when he saw me sad. He set up an automatic garden-water system so I could grow fruits and vegetables with little effort. He built a birdhouse and hung it from a backyard tree so I could bird-watch from the living room window. The list goes on. Matt always gave me his all, except his vulnerable spirit.

I can see why no one wanted to help me decide. There was no cure for a GBM, only treatments that might or might not add a few months of life. None of them sounded particularly promising or helpful. I could volunteer to be part of a clinical trial with a new drug, but they were all just experiments.

Choosing a treatment was like playing the old TV game: *Let's Make a Deal.*

Choose your hidden prize behind door number 1, door number 2, or door number 3. Contestants were always anxious to choose the best one, winning a trip to Hawaii or a new car. They didn't want to choose the wrong door and get stuck with a year's supply of laundry soap. At least it was always something good. For me, all my doors opened to roads leading to death. My three doors hid something more like this:

Door number 1: Clinical trial—snake a tube through the groin into the brain. Inject experimental chemo directly past the blood-brain barrier into the tumor cavity.

> **Risks**:   Blood clots, stroke, brain infection, seizures, death.
> **Results**: Unknown.

Door number 2: Standard treatment—Inject chemotherapy into the veins through IVs.

> **Risks**:   Brain inflammation, stroke, immune system suppression, infection, death.
> **Results**: May add three months to life while enjoying hair loss, fatigue, and nausea.

Door number 3: Wrong choice—a treatment that doesn't work for you at all.

> **Results**: Just like playing the Monopoly game and being sent past Go directly to jail. - Sent directly to death, pass Go and do not collect any days of life.

How was I to know which to choose? The doctors couldn't tell me what hid behind each door, other than my cancer was considered terminal and would lead to death sooner or later. Wasn't there a better choice? I was shafted!

I went over and over the available chemotherapy options, but always got hung up on the serious risks. It could cause so much damage to my body that it could kill me before the cancer did. After weeks of contemplating, I decided not to take chemo. Not worth it for me. If I heard the word "cure" along with "chemo" I would have considered it. All I heard was chemo equals pain and a very short extended life at best. I decided not to choose any of those doors.

I decided to let my own body fight the cancer. I figured only a few cancer cells were left in my brain after surgery. Millions of good healthy cells in my body outnumbered the bad, millions to one. Good cells had the advantage. With that ratio, they had to win! I decided to give it a shot. I would boost my own immune system and fight the cancer myself.

I mentally started attacking any remaining cancer cells. I visualized military soldiers crawling on their elbows and knees through my arteries and veins. They held rifles in their hands and looked for hidden cancer cells to destroy. When found, they blew the cancer cells to smithereens. Visualizing it was fun.

Other than a few bad GBM cells left behind after surgery, my body was healthy and ready for the challenge. "Matt, what do you think about me not taking chemotherapy and taking an herbal alternative approach?" I asked.

"Do what your heart tells you to do. It's most important that you believe in it," Matt responded.

The next week, I went to an herbalist in Ashland, Oregon, who specialized in cancer. I noticed as soon as I walked in the door that it was going to be very different from an appointment with a mainstream Western doctor. The air smelled of lavender, the aroma relaxed me. The room was quiet and inviting. A waterfall in the corner of the office tickled my ears. A huge puffy couch sat in the center of the room with a warm pot of tea nearby on a side table. The room was comforting; it calmed me. I took another deep breath of lavender.

I checked in with the smiling woman behind the front desk and sank into the warm soft couch. I closed my eyes and listened to the waterfall. Soon the herbalist, Suzanne, approached me in the waiting room to greet me. As I stood, she shook my hand gently. "Hello, Cheryl, it's nice to meet you." Then she led me to her office. Suzanne had beautiful long hair and walked as if she was gliding on a cloud.

In her office, she turned and gave me a friendly hug, then pulled out a chair for me. I'd never had a greeting like that from a doctor before. We both sat down. The week before, I had mailed her a completed ten-page questionnaire she requested, answering questions about my diet, lifestyle, and household environment.

"Please stick out your tongue," she said, then looked at it, touched it and scraped it with a tongue depressor. She quickly took notes on her laptop computer. Staring deeply into my eyes, for a long serious period of time, she took more notes. She continued asking me hundreds of questions about my eating habits, sleeping habits, menstrual cycle, on and on.

My favorite questions were the ones about my poop.

"Are your bowel movements regular and daily? Once, twice, or three times a day? Is it soft or hard? Does it sink or float? Is the color light or dark? Does it stink or not smell at all?"

I felt uncomfortable and embarrassed, even though she asked them sweetly. I couldn't help but visualize her standing next to me in the bathroom while I sat on the toilet. My heart beat fast, my face flushed, and I squirmed on the chair. After the intense interview, she gave me a long list of herbal supplements she recommended. Even though I couldn't pronounce the Chinese names or understand how they helped, I chose to move ahead. I spent hundreds of dollars purchasing bottles of liquid drops, capsules, teas, and powders.

Back in the car, I set the bag loaded with herbs in the passenger seat. They smelled nasty even through the packaging! I stuck the car in gear and drove off. *I can handle the herbal stink better than chemo pain.*

I'd seen people take herbal supplements in the past and thought they were ignorant and crazy. I never dreamed it would be me choking down over sixty capsules a day. I took supplements before meals, during meals, and at bedtime—overall, seven times a day. My life revolved around the supplement schedule.

Eating out was hard, always carrying a purse full of supplements. I poured them out on the restaurant table and tried to sneak them down so others couldn't see. If I gulped them too quickly, they'd stick in my throat and I would need to drink more and more water to force them down. My stomach filled with water, leaving little room for food.

I often wanted to throw them away, but fear of the GBM coming back motivated me to keep choking them down. Over time it got to be routine, like taking a shower or brushing my teeth.

Eventually, I did it without thought. There was no proof that it would save my life, but I felt good that I was actively doing something. Above all, the natural herbal approach didn't cause the bad side effects the chemo would.

CHAPTER 7

AWAY WITH THE MASK OF THE PAST

For almost two months, I had been faithfully taking herbal supplements. I had refused to take chemotherapy, but my neuro-oncologist still pushed me to consider taking traditional Western treatments. I held firm that I didn't want chemo, but began considering radiation.

According to statistics, radiation, like chemotherapy, only added a few months of life; but radiation didn't seem as scary to me. My radiologist told me that it was not painful and didn't have horrible side effects. You lie on a table. *Zip, zap, boom.* And it's over.

UCSF was conducting a radiation clinical trial at that time, an experiment looking for a "cure". The clinical trial called for standard radiation with an addition of extra oxygen during the treatment. The pharmaceutical company agreed to cover the cost of a hotel and gas for a two-month stay in California for the trial.

That sounded reasonable to me. It was like getting a free vacation! Well, sort of.

After living in small rural towns my whole life, the thought of spending time in a vibrant metropolis was intriguing. Crossing the Golden Gate Bridge, walking along the wharf, and exploring Chinatown made a few months in San Francisco sound like fun.

I also knew I needed some quiet time alone to think about changes I needed to make in my lifestyle. Recently I had read Albert Einstein's definition of "insanity": "Doing he same thing over and over again and expecting different results." A light bulb clicked on in my mind.

Something in my past lifestyle led to brain cancer. The way I lived in the past was not healthy for me. If I don't want cancer to return, I must make changes. I can't do the same things over again and expect different results.

At home, living the same routine, it was hard to see out of the box. I was willing to be separated from my family temporarily in hopes it would give me time alone to focus on finding my own personal "cure" to brain cancer. Short-term separation from family could help lead to more time with them in the long run.

I decided to move ahead with the UCSF radiation clinical trail and headed south to San Francisco. I loaded my van with everything I needed for a two-month stay, including my mountain bike. I visualized the trip as a fun and new step forward in life. Driving with the window rolled down and warm wind blowing through my hair, I actually had a smile on my face.

My mom and Pat (Mema and Pappy) volunteered to take care of Grant and Clint for the two months. They lived only two and a half hours from UCSF, so I could spend time with the boys on the weekends.

Pappy and Mema

Pappy with Grant and Clint

Matt stayed home in Oregon, working full-time and taking care of our remaining pets: Butterfinger, our pony; Tulip, our goat; Susie, Shasta, and Tok, our sled dogs; Amber, Matt's hunting dog; two turkeys; and over fifteen laying hens.

I found a Bay Area home for myself, an old but well-kept hotel across the street from the San Francisco Zoo. When I cracked open the window to get the smell of the ocean, it sounded like an African savannah. Lions roared, elephants trumpeted; and all together, the zoo animals bellowed during their feeding time. As a biologist, I loved lying on the bed, identifying animals by sound.

The room had a small kitchen with a sink, dishes, a little refrigerator, and a microwave. I shopped at the nearby organic grocery store and cooked my own healthy meals.

The hotel was only two blocks from the ocean and five miles from the hospital. I rode my bike to UCSF for treatment each day. The ten-mile round-trip strengthened me, even while undergoing radiation. I had recently read Lance Armstrong's book *It's Not About the Bike,* and it inspired me to push myself like Lance did during his treatments.

54

Early each morning, riding my bike along the beach path overlooking the ocean, I headed north to UCSF. With each deep breath, I could smell the ocean and hear the sound of the waves. Pumping my muscles as hard as I could, I strengthened physically and emotionally. The hard exercise made me feel indestructible, empowered, and energized. *Cancer can't kill me, I'm too strong!* I would think as I pedaled.

I couldn't help but smile while biking along, so thankful I was capable of it. I knew many brain tumor patients were partially disabled and didn't have the ability to ride their bikes and exercise. I felt blessed.

After three miles along the beach, the path turned east into the Golden Gate Park. A paved trail swerved and headed slightly uphill, passing under beautiful huge trees. Breezes blew the smell of eucalyptus trees into the air, and with each deep breath, I felt cleansed. Uncountable colors and shades of green danced through the bushes, trees, and small ground covers. I was biking through an amazing botanical garden. I heard the birds singing, agreeing with me in my love for the park and for life.

Leaving the park, I turned south and headed up the slope to the hospital. The incline was so steep my thighs burned as I pushed to make it up the hill. Out of breath at the top, I got off the bike, leaned back against the hospital's cool concrete wall, and closed my eyes. I was physically tired and at the same time deeply happy, convinced the bike ride each morning had to be better for my health than any doctor's medical treatments!

At the hospital, I parked my bike at the main entrance. With my helmet still on and my backpack thrown over my shoulder, I strode confidently into the radiation waiting room. Plopping down on an uncomfortable stiff chair, I glanced around and smiled at the others. Most looked worn down and twenty to forty years older than me.

More than once a patient asked, "Are you a medical student?"

I couldn't help but smile and say, "No, I'm a cancer patient too." Usually I would hear, "You look too healthy, you can't have cancer!"

I would smile, relax, lean back, and think to myself, *Yes, I am a healthy person, and I'll stay that way.* I felt alive!

The radiation clinical trial used an experimental medication called H-boc. It was actually cow hemoglobin. The nurse was to inject me with the H-boc each morning before the radiation, five days a week for a six-week period. In the past, I never imagined becoming part cow and often joked with the nurse, mooing while she injected me.

A week before the trial began; a Port-a-Cath was implanted in my chest located directly under my skin on the right side near my collarbone. A tube traveled from the entrance of the port through a vein and straight into my heart, making injection faster and easier. The nurse used the Port-a-Cath to inject the H-boc. I was so glad to have a port because I was sick of being poked in my arm over and over. Before the port was installed, I probably looked like a drug user with bruises all over my veins in the crook of my arms.

Hemoglobin is the part of red blood cells that carries oxygen throughout your body. My blood's ability to carry oxygen was super-sized by the H-boc. I bet professional athletes would be jealous. During radiation, I was given pure oxygen through a mask. My blood oxygen level skyrocketed way above normal range. I lay there and wished I could jump on my bike and ride. Surely I could keep up with Lance Armstrong with my supercharged oxygen level.

Cancer cells create an inflamed environment around them, which reduces oxygen availability to nearby normal cells. This lack of oxygen to cells is called hypoxia and inhibits normal cells from fighting off cancer cells. It also allows some cancer cells to hide out in a dormant state. Radiation kills cancer cells only when they are growing and dividing. If they're dormant, they can sneak past radiation and grow later. H-boc was supposed to stimulate dormant cancer cells to grow so that radiation could successfully kill them. I never thought one of my doctors' goals would be to speed up the cancer growth!

After H-boc was injected, I quickly headed to the radiation oncology department for the next step. A mask, made from rigid plastic mesh that had been custom molded to my face, was placed over my skull and bolted to the table to hold my head perfectly still during brain radiation.

Once secured to the table, a huge, thick lead door slammed closed, sealing off the radiation room I was in from the rest of the hospital and other people. I was alone. I'm not claustrophobic, but when bolted to the table and left alone in the room, I began to panic. My heart began pounding so hard, I thought it would jump out of my chest.

The technicians spoke to me over an intercom from a nearby room, "Are you ready?" The treatment would take about fifteen minutes, but each second felt like hours. I wondered what would happen if a big earthquake hit the Bay Area while I was locked to the table. I figured everyone would quickly evacuate the building, leaving me behind as the building crumbled to the ground.

To control the panic, I followed advice from a friend and escaped mentally to a "happy home." During my first radiation treatment, and then repeatedly each time after that, when the lead door slam closed, I'd shut my eyes and cleared my mind to find that place.

It came to my mind came quickly: I stood on the peak of a huge, pointed, rocky mountain. The sky was covered with dark purple-and-pink clouds. A heavy wind blew, moving the clouds quickly across the sky. A huge electrical storm flashed lightning above me, but I heard no thunder or wind, only quietness.

I was wearing a sleek long silky dress, which fluttered gracefully in the wind. The air felt warm and comforting. I was at peace even though the atmosphere around me was deep, dark, and uncontrollable. I was not scared; I knew God was up there.

I leaned forward into the wind and stretched my arms up to him. My fingers almost touched his as he reached down toward me. I felt an urge to jump from the mountaintop. Without thinking, or worrying about falling to my death, I leaped. God's warm wind held me up, and I glided out over the valley below. I felt love and peace, knowing I was taken care of. No fear. Flying and looking down at the beautiful valley, I knew God would always be with me.

With a loud click and the sound of heavy sliding metal, the lead door opened. My consciousness returned to the radiation table. When the technician unhooked and removed my mask, I sat up and stretched, so happy that the visualization technique worked.

From that point on, I used visualization whenever I had to go through hard times. It helped me during each radiation treatment and also when I went through the numerous MRI tests I would endure during my battle.

The H-boc treatment didn't last the expected six weeks. Two weeks into the trial, on a Friday afternoon, I was driving to Mom and Pat's home to spend the weekend with the boys. At a Taco Bell drive-through, I ordered a Pepsi and a bean burrito with no onions. Pulling back onto the highway, I took a sip from the straw, but couldn't swallow it. My throat was tight, the Pepsi was stuck, and I panicked. Setting the soda aside, I drove as fast as I could to Yuba City, an hour away.

Unfortunately, I couldn't go to my "happy home" while driving, having to keep my eyes on the road. All I did was worry that my tumor was coming back.

By the time I got to my mom and Pat's house, most of the capillaries in my skin, on my legs, and arms had burst, turning my tan skin into a bloody red. Pat calmed me down and said, "I'll take you to the emergency room."

It was great being with him. He is always calm, no matter what happens around him. I remember one night, when I was still in high school, the doorbell rang at about two o'clock. Pat, my mom, and all of us kids jumped out of bed and ran to the front door, wondering who would be there in the middle of the night. Pat opened the door; and there stood a police officer, beside him was my little brother, Scott, still in junior high. The policeman pushed Scott forward toward us and said, "I caught him running around the neighborhood, looking like he was up to no good."

Pat thanked the police officer, closed the door, and told us all to go back to bed. We kids just stood there in wonder. We all expected Pat to lose his cool and yell at Scott, but he just turned around and walked back to his bedroom with my mom following him. Early the next morning, at five o'clock, Pat got up to go to work at his rice-and-tomato ranch. He calmly pulled Scott out of bed and drove him out to the fields with him. Scott was required to work hard in the fields all day, with only three hours of sleep the night before. Pat never once lost his temper or yelled, but he sure got his point across.

On the way to the emergency room, I lay back in the passenger seat next to Pat. I closed my eyes and took a deep breath. Pat's calm persona weaved its way into me.

The doctor in the ER said I was having an allergic reaction to the H-boc. He gave me a shot and sent me home saying, "In a week or so, the redness will go away." I was happy that my face wasn't blood-red too.

That next Monday, back at UCSF, I got kicked off the clinical trial. I couldn't continue the H-boc after my allergic reaction. My neuro-oncologist warned, "Be cautious the next time you eat beef, you could have an allergic reaction to it too." In fear, I completely cut out beef from my diet for years.

After only three weeks in San Francisco, I went home to finish standard radiation at a local hospital in Medford, Oregon. I was disappointed that my Bay Area "vacation" had been cut short, but happy that at least I'd had a little quiet time alone.

I'd spent hours each day sitting cross-legged on my comfortable hotel-room bed or outside in the Golden Gate Park under the beautiful trees. After hours of deep thought, conversations with God, and time in the Bible, I'd started to visualize what my new lifestyle back in Oregon should look like to win my battle against cancer. It would take a complete 180-degree turn from my old lifestyle. I was excited about what was to come.

CHAPTER 8

ONE HOME TO ANOTHER

On my way back to Oregon, I stopped at my mom and Pat's house to pick up the boys. I thanked them for taking care of the boys. As Grant, Clint, and I loaded into the van, we hugged Mema and Pappy good-bye and then drove home, looking forward to giving Daddy big hugs too.

Five hours later, we pulled into the long driveway. Matt must have heard the crunching of the gravel under the tires because he rushed out to greet us. I unhooked the boys' car seats as fast as I could. We all gave Matt big hugs, happy to be home together.

Later that night, after Matt and I tucked the boys in bed, I said, "We need to talk." After spending three weeks in California, thinking hard, I wanted to talk with Matt about changes I felt we should make to strengthen our family. If the Broyles family in the future became only Matt, Grant, and Clint, I wanted to make it as easy on them as possible. I wanted Matt and me to prepare for my possible death. Just the thought that they could be OK if I was gone gave me a little peace.

Matt didn't like talking about cancer and me possibly dying from it. The topic was taboo. He didn't want to open his tear faucet and ruin the happy feeling of me being home. "Do we have to talk about it tonight?"

I, on the other hand, was in the mood for moving ahead with solutions to the potential problems I saw. I wanted to make sure my family was protected. I was anxious to dive into the subject, hold each other tight, and cry together.

"There are some changes I think we should make," I said once we settled on the couch. I could see the hesitant expression on his face, but I pressed ahead. "In case I'm not here in the future, I think you should be the one to tuck the boys into bed at night from now on so they could get used to you doing it."

I had always been the one who brushed Grant and Clint's teeth, read them books, and tucked them in bed at night, with hugs and kisses. I had learned from reading some hospice documents that bedtime was the most difficult time of day for children with lost loved ones. He nodded and swallowed hard. The pain of the topic was there, and we both cried together.

"Also, can you please start paying the monthly bills and yearly taxes with me, so you can learn the routine and won't have to struggle through it for the first time, if I'm gone?" Matt nodded. We both continued to cry.

Sinking deeper into the couch and holding each other tight, we talked late into the night. We talked about Matt's work schedule and how it would change if I died, about who would take care of the boys when he was at work. What if he needed to travel out of town for meetings? We talked about all the "what ifs" and tried to plan solutions. Late at night, we finally went to bed, emotionally strung out.

Later that week, I opened another can of worms. Since I had stopped working a few months before, our income had been cut in half. We'd been using my work disability compensation and savings to cover the loss of my salary, but that would only last so long. I worried about whether we would be able to pay for future medical bills and the mortgage. I didn't want the bank to foreclose our property, leaving us homeless.

After the boys were tucked in bed, I pulled Matt over to the couch. "We need to talk again." We both sat down and delved into the taboo. "I think we should sell our house and move to a less expensive one in town. We can't afford to stay here. Also, if I weren't here, how would you work a full-time job, take care of thirty-two acres, two little boys, one goat, four dogs, one pony, two turkeys, and fifteen chickens?" I paused. "We need to downsize and simplify our lives."

The house on Griffin Lane as seen from the road (1994)

I could see from the look in Matt's eyes, he agreed and saw the logic of it, but I also saw his dreams come tumbling down. We'd both had dreams of retiring one day, surrounded by our own little old-growth forest with a spotted owl hooting at us from the backyard. When the dream crashed, he would lose his forest and might lose his wife too. With a deep breath, Matt finally spoke, "I agree, let's do it." Again, we held each other tight and continued to talk until late into the night. Talking seriously about the possibility of my death seemed unreal—detached form reality. But we needed to. Later, we went to bed with a plan.

Matt and I have always been fast movers. Type A personalities. When we decided to do something, we'd do it quickly. A confident planner, I decided to sell the house myself. I was sure I could do a more cost-effective and faster job than a real-estate agent. I couldn't swallow the idea of paying a large agent fee.

It had been four months since my surgery in June, and I had just finished radiation. Fall was coming, and we wanted to complete the move before the winter holiday season. Matt and I planned and hoped for a fast sale and purchase.

But we had some problems. Over the six years of living on thirty-two acres with a barn, we had collected a lot of things that wouldn't fit into a smaller house. Also, life had been so hectic after I was diagnosed that we had stopped all yard maintenance. Leaves, pine needles, cones, weeds, and dog poop had built up over the months. The place wouldn't sell fast if it didn't look pretty. We needed some help.

The next weekend, ten of my former coworkers at Boise Cascade showed up. They worked hard all day—mowing lawns, raking the leaves, and pulling weeds. They sprayed all the dust and cobwebs off the house sidings. They cleaned needles out of the rain gutters. They hauled eight pickup loads of stuff to the dump and Goodwill. They helped remodel an office Matt had been working on. At the end of the day, they each gave me a hug and left with a huge weight taken off our shoulders. I was so blessed to have great loyal friends. I knew we all respected each other and were good comrades at work, but I never knew they cared enough to reach out and help me that way.

Cheryl's friends from Boise Cascade: Brian, Ken, and Ken hanging drywall at Griffin Lane Home

Friends from the Bureau of Land Management office, where Matt had worked for over ten years, helped too. Frances came and took Tulip, our goat, home with her. Jeannine hauled off all the chickens. They both told us they would "pet-sit" for us in case we wanted the critters back in the future.

Matt and I also knew that all our dogs could not live with us in town. We decided to keep only one. Shasta was my favorite sled dog, and I couldn't bear being without her. We put ads in the newspaper trying to find homes for the other three dogs—Tok, Susie, and Amber, Matt's hunting dog.

People responded quickly on ads for Tok and Susie. Two families came and took them away. No one responded to Amber's ad. She was a pit-bull-and-golden-lab mix, our only non sled dog. Matt had gotten her his last year in college. Even though she ended up not being a good retriever, Matt loved her. Instead of retrieving a game bird, Amber would pick it up and shake it, feathers flying everywhere. (We figured it was the pit bull in her.) In her old age, she'd gotten deaf, senile, grumpy, and protective of her food. The Humane Society wouldn't even take her. We couldn't trust her around Grant and Clint in a small house in town. Finally, I got brave enough and brought her to our vet to euthanize her. I didn't want Matt to have to do that job again. Grant and Clint were in tears seeing all our pets going away.

Since my diagnosis, my dad and Red really reached out to me. One blessing of cancer was that we had grown closer, and our love for each other poured out. They knew the boys were mourning about losing their pets. Out of the sweetness of their hearts, they drove north five hours from California to Oregon with a horse trailer and took our pony Butterfinger home with them. The boys were relieved to know they could see Butterfinger again when they visited Grandma Gin and Grandpa Will.

Watching our pets and truckloads of personal stuff hauled away had a dual effect on me. Part was sadness to see it all go. My dream was crushed. No farm pets, no sled dog team, no forest growing into an old-growth rich ecosystem, no property where the boys could explore and play in the wild outdoors. It was all gone.

Grandma Gin (Red) and Grandpa Will

At the same time, I felt a heavy weight lifted off my shoulders. All the things we lost had taken a lot of work to manage. In a small house in town, our family's life would be simplified with more time to relax. I've always loved the excitement of change too. What would our new house look like? What fun would the boys and I have together now that I was at home full-time with them? The thought of a new simple life was comforting.

Our house sold within a week, and we found another just as quickly. Grant is actually the one who chose it. I remember him saying, "This is the one. I'm not leaving." His decision was based on an amazing fort in the backyard. It had a window view that covered the whole backyard and the neighbors' too. It was pink. I was surprised he wanted one painted with what he considered a girl's color. It must have been the trapdoor in the floor, the room for two sleeping bags, and the beautiful grapevines that surrounded it that convinced him. Grant did insist that we repaint it in camouflage pattern right away.

The fort at the Glenn Way house

What convinced me that it should be our new home were the three raised garden beds. I couldn't have chickens in town, but I could have a mini-vegetable garden. There was room in the beds to plant peas, broccoli, zucchini, squash, lettuce, and, my favorite, strawberries. I envisioned myself working in the garden while listening to the boys giggling in the fort nearby. I looked down at Grant and said, "Yes, this is the place."

We made an offer to the owners right then and there. They accepted it immediately. They too were selling their home themselves, and we sealed the agreement with the shake of our hands. There was something comforting about that.

We made significant profit selling our larger home on acreage. The real-estate money, along with my retirement money, was almost enough to completely pay for the small house in town, without a mortgage. All we needed was forty thousand dollars. Matt's grandparents, Gummy and Gumpy, offered to loan us the money interest free, and we could repay them over a time period that we could afford. We were so appreciative. To own a home without a mortgage was comforting. We didn't have to worry about ending up in the gutter.

Matt and I were also amazed at how smoothly and quickly things changed. Within what seemed like the blink of an eye, we sold our old house, closed on the purchase of our new house, and moved in. We met our own personal goal and settled into the new home by Thanksgiving. We knew it wasn't just luck or coincidence; God was helping us. Since my diagnosis, I had noticed too many unexpected miracles to think it was all luck. My hope for the future rested in God's hands. I felt confident I would see more miracles in my life to come.

Life in the little town home was wonderful. The boys had fun playing in the neighborhood park. We all loved taking walks around the blocks. Grant practiced riding his little tricycle as I pushed Clint in a stroller.

Grant on his bike in our new neighborhood

They both played in the fort and on the backyard swing set, and I loved sitting in a comfortable chair watching the boys play. Since we were not so busy taking care of all the numerous pets and the thirty-two acres anymore, Matt had time to take the boys fishing on the weekends and teach them how to put worms on the hook and cast their poles. Being a stay-at-home mom, I didn't have to worry anymore about missing the boys' firsts. I was there to hear Clint's first words and to see Grant drawing his beautiful pictures. Our family was so happy.

Five months had passed since I was diagnosed with brain cancer, and I was still alive! According to statistics, I had only eight more months to go. I often sat by the window looking out into space, contemplating what more I could do to fight cancer. I wanted years of wonderful time with my family, not months.

I've gone through surgery, radiation, started taking herbal supplements, quit my job, moved into a small relaxing home . . . What else can I do? I want to live many healthy years.

I started doing more research, trying to find more ways to battle and win the war against cancer. I prayed and knew God would help me find the way.

CHAPTER 9

LIVING HEALTHY AND WHOLE

Thanksgiving and Christmas came and went. I prayed to God that I would be alive to celebrate the next holiday season with my family. Often during the winter dark season, people look deep inside themselves. Then on New Year's Day, set new goals for themselves for the coming year. In the past, I'd always wished for things like losing weight, saving for a new car or a vacation to Hawaii. Now my life was different. My New Year's goal for 2001 was just to be alive.

Dark winter anxieties and stress erupted in Matt's daily life as a husband to a cancer patient and a wildlife biologist battling with foresters about timber harvest. After observing him in a state of anger at work, his supervisor realized he was a time bomb ready to explode. He needed to be defused. Matt was required to go to a weeklong workshop called Personal Effectiveness Seminar (PES) at WINGS, the innovative learning group in Eugene, Oregon. It was not as a suggestion, but an order.

He was angry about being forced to attend the workshop. As a manly man, he couldn't stand the thought of going to a place called WINGS. "WINGS—I'm probably going to run into fairies fluttering around," Matt fumed, his face red in anger as he filled his suitcase.

Sitting on the bed next to him, packing, I laughed. "Are you scared of fairies?"

Matt stomped out of the room and headed to Eugene. He came back another person. His changed demeanor shocked me. Matt was actually smiling. He even looked different. The muscles in his face were relaxed. The frustrated wrinkled forehead was gone.

Some winged fairy must have sprinkled some magic dust on him. "Matt, what happened at WINGS? What did you learn?" I asked, along with a million other questions.

All he would say was, "You have to find out for yourself." I wasn't going to argue with that. *I wanted some magical dust too.* Soon afterward, I packed my bag and headed to Eugene.

What I experienced in PES was amazing. We all learned techniques that showed us the goodness and love within ourselves and how to access them. Each of us went in as one person and came out as another. We all walked out with an afterglow, our eyes shining, smiles sparkling, and skin glowing. We were happy new people.

This was different from the happiness and glow you get when you visit Disneyland or take a trip to Hawaii. This was a glow that comes from within and can last forever, not like a tan that fades over time. Our WINGS instructor took a picture of each of us, to bring home, because she wanted everyone to remember it.

The most significant thought that came back repeatedly when I got home was something my instructor told me, "You are what you think you are." She had taken my hands one day and pulled me aside and said, "If you think you're sick, you will be. If you think you're healthy, you will be. Your mind has strength." At home, I realized I needed to convince my body it was cancer free.

I started with some of the easiest changes I could make, physical ones. I bought an elliptical exercise machine and began working out more than thirty minutes a day, five days a week. When the sweat rolled down my forehead, I visualized it as any remaining cancer cells pouring out. I hiked, ran, biked, swam, skated, skied—did everything to keep my body moving—convinced Lance Armstrong did so well fighting cancer because he had pushed himself physically. If I thought of myself as a healthy strong athlete, I would be one. The more I moved, the healthier I felt.

Next I changed my diet. In the past, Matt and I spent so much time working we didn't have time to eat healthy meals. Every few weeks, we shopped at Costco and loaded up with unhealthy prepared frozen foods filled with MSG, sodium nitrates, fake sugars, and many other additives and preservatives. After doing research on cancer, I realized those ingredients could make you sick and possibly kill you. I needed to cleanse my body and boost my immune system to fight the cancer. I decided to switch to healthy organic foods.

I tried to consume eight to ten servings of fruits and vegetables a day with as many colors as I could grab—red, green, yellow, purple, and orange—to fill my body with antioxidants. Each morning, I made juice by grinding up an apple, broccoli, carrots, and kale. It may sound disgusting, but it actually tasted pretty good. However, I could never convince Grant or Clint to drink it.

Matt after a successful turkey hunt

I cut out heavy, fatty meats and switched to fish, chicken, and wild game. In the past, I didn't fully appreciate the game Matt shot and brought home. But after researching recommendations on cancer diets, I realized how healthy it was.

Elk, deer, duck, trout, and other wildlife eat natural insects and greens, unlike domestic animals like cows that eat processed corn and are filled with hormones and antibiotics. Instead of being

71

filled with bad fats and chemicals, eating food from the wild filled us with healthy omega-3 fats.

We bought another freezer and started stocking both freezers up with as much wild game Matt could bring home. My sister Jenny and her husband, Mark, a professional fisherman in Alaska, sent us pounds and pounds of freshly frozen wild salmon and cod. We were stocked up with good organic protein.

I moved from simple carbohydrates like white bread and rice to whole grains and food with more fiber. The hardest thing was cutting out sugar. I've always had a sweet tooth, but learned that if I ate sugar, it would raise my blood glucose level and feed the cancer. Cancer cells metabolize glucose fifteen times faster than normal cells. So I cut out the sugar and tried to starve the cancer. Any time a candy bar called out to me and I reached out for it, I felt like I was killing myself. That thought alone motivated me to push it aside— most of the time.

At times I would get resentful, especially at birthday parties and holidays where everyone else ate cake and ice cream. *How can they eat this in front of me! They would never drink alcohol right in front of an alcoholic.* I would often stomp away and hide by myself in a far-off room. Later, I found alternatives. I love strawberries and other fresh fruits that are just as yummy as processed white sugar. I started bringing my own treats when I attended parties and places where people would be eating sugar right under my nose.

After putting a lot of effort into strengthening my body, I still didn't feel whole and complete. There remained an empty spot. After more deep thought, I came to realize strengthening my soul was just as important as strengthening my physical body. I had to take another step forward.

I gathered and read as many books as I could find about living healthy. My three favorite ones that helped me shape my new entity were the Bible, the book *Love, Medicine and Miracles* by Dr. Bernie S. Siegel, and *Spontaneous Healing* by Dr. Andrew Weil. I studied each page, took notes, planned, and dreamed. Each day, I evolved a little more.

In the past, I'd started each morning with a pen in my hand making a list of all the things I needed to do that day, and then rushed around trying to get everything done. All I could think about or notice was the next thing on my list. Not resting, sapped my energy and left me empty. I had no fulfilled feeling in my soul.

In my new life, I began every morning on my knees in prayer. Giving time to God and searching for wisdom, I was fueled. With a full tank, I felt energized, stronger, and wiser. Finally I understood the Bible's teaching that God can give you peace that surpasses understanding.

I also set time aside each day to be still, clearing my mind and listening to what my soul or God might tell me. Quiet time and deep breathing renewed me. In the past, I'd always rushed around like I was running out of time, speed-walking from one chore to the next. I would never sit down and relax.

At work I had supervised Kim, a fisheries biologist, and Tim, a wildlife biologist. I remembered them telling me I was a workaholic. My new quiet time at home gave me a new perspective that changed from "hurry, hurry, I've got to get it done" to "relax, I have all the time in the world." I slowed down and began doing things with ease.

Using the teachings from WINGS, I realized my thoughts had power. "You are what you think you are" was so true. If I chose to be happy, I was. It was my choice, regardless of the circumstances I was in. Sadness and fear overcame me only if I let it. In the past, I would let my sadness and anger brew and bubble deep inside, getting worse until it boiled over.

Often Matt and the boys would be the ones spilled on and burned. I remembered losing patience with Grant and Clint and yelling no or stop, when all they did was accidentally knock over a glass of milk. Putting mind over matter, I overcame the weakness. I chose to be happy each day no matter what happened and began rolling with the waves of daily life. I lived in the moment and didn't worry about the past or the future. Living spontaneously with laughs was my goal.

I e-mailed everyone on my address list and asked them what they thought was the funniest movie they ever saw. No more scary movies for me, only ones that would make me laugh. Research indicated that laughing boosted your immune system. I figured each laugh could locate and take out any remaining hidden cancer cells. With everyone's responses, I made a long list of movies to watch. Joe, Matt's dad, recommended Peter Sellers's Pink Panther movies.

Matt, the boys, and I spent many evenings laughing and bouncing around on the couch watching them.

I started to notice and enjoy all the little things around me I'd rarely noticed in the past—feeling the warm sun on my cheek, smelling the flowers in the air, hearing the sound of a bumblebee flying by, enjoying the sweet taste of an apple. My perception progressed from two-dimensional black-and-white to an amazing beautiful multicolored three-dimensional panorama.

In the past, when I took Grant and Clint to play at a park, I would only see the boys and think about their safety. I often looked down at my watch and counted the time until we needed to leave. My eyes followed them, but I wouldn't notice anything else. Now, I saw things differently. It was as if the neurosurgeon hadn't cut out a chunk from my brain, but added something special to it. I would sit back and see Grant and Clint playing with joy and giggling. I would laugh with them. I would look up and see the stunning white cumulus clouds in the blue sky. I noticed other people around me and would actually have conversations with them. I would never even think to look down at my watch.

I also read the book *Clear Your Clutter with Feng Shui*. Author, Karen Kingston, recommended I free myself from physical, mental, emotional, and spiritual clutter around the house. First, I got rid of stuff stored and shoved under our bed. Then I moved to the closet and got rid of all the clothes I hadn't worn in the last year. Walking around the house, I allowed myself to get rid of gifts people had given me over the years that I didn't even like—a book on the shelf, shoes in the closet, a picture on the wall, a bowl in the kitchen, or a set of earrings in my jewelry box. If it didn't make me happy to see it, I got rid of it. As clutter was removed, I walked a little lighter and bounced a little higher with each step.

My family relationships also transformed. In the past, on the weekends, Matt and I focused on chores that needed to be done or bills that needed to be paid—no thoughts of relaxing or having fun. That often led to arguments in front of our boys. "You forgot to pay the f—— bills, not me!" "Get your d—— dirty socks off the floor, you do the laundry!" "I'm going fishing, you get the cars' oil changed" were the common arguments the boys heard.

My perspective changed on what was important in life, and slowly, my whole family changed along with me. We realized nothing was more important than reaching out and loving others. We started having more conversations expressing love: "Thank you for mowing the lawn today!" "Can I help you do the dishes?" "I love you so much."

In the past, love was hard for me to express because of fears of being rejected or being vulnerable. I used to agree with the song "What's Love Got to Do with It" by Tina Turner, about how love can break your heart. That's how I felt. But then, seeing life anew, I realized if I didn't show my love, my heart would shrivel up and blow away. If you don't use it, you lose it.

Slowly, I opened up to love. I started to have the strength to tear down the wall I had built over the years. It wasn't easy. Sometimes I still crawled back into the little hidden crack in the remaining bricks of the wall. But at least I realized that love was healing and wouldn't hurt me. I stepped forward; I started experimenting with love.

I hugged friends and family when they were within arm's reach and told them I loved them. When I walked around town, I looked at people directly in their eyes and drew their sight back to me. I said hello and would give them a big smile and hoped they recognized they were noticed and loved. I relished each time I saw a frown turn into a smile. It was like my joy reached out and touched them.

I stopped to assist people I saw needing help—reaching for something on a store shelf for an elderly person, opening a door for someone with full arms, or picking up something a person had dropped.

I reached out to a fifteen year old teenage girl, Jennifer Royse, who had lost her mother to breast cancer when she was ten. I noticed her at church one Sunday morning when she was fifteen.

She wore black clothes, black lipstick, and more than twenty rings. I talked with the church's youth pastor and found out about her history. She was suffering and had threatened suicide at one point. My heart went out to her. I wanted her to feel love. I walked up to her one day after church and tapped her on her shoulder.

"Hello, my name is Cheryl, and I was hoping we could get to know one another. Would you like to go out to dinner with me sometime?"

The look on her face was breathtaking. Her eyes glowed, and she smiled and said, "Yes, I'd like that."

That first night at dinner, we clicked, and we began doing things together each week. I reached out with love to her, and she sucked it in. She became the daughter I never had, and we've stayed close ever since.

Cheryl and Jennifer Royse at 18 years old

Showing love to others didn't hurt; it energized me. Each time I reached out to show love to others, I felt empowered and strengthened deep inside. My mind finally understood God's advice: A life lived without expressing love adds up to nothing.

With my new life, I got stronger each day, both physically and emotionally. I looked, felt, and acted healthier the year after being diagnosed with cancer than I did before.

I never would have thought cancer could be a blessing.

CHAPTER 10

FOUR YEARS LATER

Four years passed, and I was still alive! They had been the best years of my life.

I'd been there to hear Clint's first words, "mom" and "dog." I cheered Grant on at his first soccer game. We had so much fun together those four years after diagnosis. We threw snowballs in the winter, went bird-watching in the spring, camped along rivers in the summer, and picked up fallen leaves in the fall. Life was great.

The doctors didn't think I'd make it past a year. I felt like I'd won the bet where the odds were against me. Surgery and radiation had caused some notable and irritating memory and cognitive problems, but nothing I couldn't live with and still enjoy life. I never would've guessed that life after cancer would be better than before.

When Grant turned five and hit kindergarten, I decided to homeschool. I couldn't bear the thought of being separated from him all day. I taught him to count and say his alphabet. We worked with shapes and colors. Clint had fun playing along with us.

Every few months I headed south to UCSF for an MRI. About a week before each trip, anxiety built up in Matt and me. I call it PMS, a type both male and female have, pre-MRI syndrome. It's worse than the normal female hormonal PMS. The closer I got to the MRI machine, the worse the PMS hit me.

Usually Matt stayed home with the boys, and my best friend from high school, Deena, went to San Francisco with me. She was such a blessing. We ended up talking about anything and nothing and giggling like we did together as teenage girls. Each MRI trip turned into a fun time. I'd end up getting good news that the scan was clear, no tumor seen. Then Deena and I would celebrate by going out to eat and then watching a good chick flick together.

One time, after my MRI trip, I returned home to find Grant and Clint's dirty underwear sitting on the backyard porch, but where were they? The underwear were no longer white, but a mixture of brown, green, and black. Then I heard Matt and the boys laughing, and I looked up to find them hiding behind the freshly painted fort. Matt and the boys had been busy those last few days. They had painted over the pinkish purple and replaced it with a camouflage. They rushed forward and gave me a wonderful welcome with big hugs and kisses. Matt had allowed the boys to paint only in their underwear so they wouldn't ruin their clothes. By the time I arrived, he had washed the boys squeaky clean so they could all surprise me with hugs when I got home.

The spring of 2003, Matt and I bought a twenty-four-foot-long camping trailer. Being a wilderness backpacker, I never thought I would own a trailer and camp in a park like RV campground setting. With small children, life had changed.

Matt and I decided to take a six-week trip around the United States in our trailer. Grant was six and Clint, four. It was a fun learning experience for all of us. We headed south through California, then east into Arizona and along the Gulf of Mexico until we hit Florida. We saw the Carlsbad Caverns in New Mexico, walked through the beautiful pecan forests of Texas, ate the delicious crawdads in Louisiana, and got bitten by hundreds of insects in the Okefenokee Swamp of Georgia. Then we headed north, driving up through the Great Smoky Mountains of North Carolina down through the Shenandoah Valley of Virginia, fished the lakes of Pennsylvania, and stopped to camp in New Hampshire for a few days to visit Matt's family.

Then we headed west and got soaked at Niagara Falls, then continued west and camped along the shores of Lake Erie; we ate lunch in the Amish region of Indiana, visited Matt's uncle's family in Wisconsin, and watched bison in the Blue Mounds of Minnesota. Our favorite part of the trip was our stay in the Black Hills of South Dakota—visiting Mount Rushmore and the Crazy Horse Memorial, watching fossils being dug at the Mammoth Site, and petting huge tortoises at the Reptile Gardens. We could have settled in there and lived in the Black Hills; it was beautiful.

Our timeline required us to keep moving. We watched paleontologists dig fossils at Wyoming Dinosaur Center and saw moose in Grand Teton National Park. We went bird-watching along the Snake River in Idaho and climbed down into a lava cave at the Newberry National Volcanic Monument back in Oregon. It was a trip we will never forget.

That fall, Matt approached me and asked, "What do you think about moving again?" He had been given an opportunity to transfer from the Medford BLM office to the one in Klamath Falls, east of the Cascade Mountains. Matt had been working in the Rogue Valley for over thirteen years and was ready for a change. He wanted to work with different wildlife species and habitats. He was also worn-out working as a wildlife biologist in politically volatile BLM district that focused on timber production. The Klamath Falls office was smaller and provided a more laid-back atmosphere.

I wanted Matt and our family to be happy. I knew Klamath Falls in Oregon was no further away from my neuro-oncologist in San Francisco or my family in Yuba City, California. So that location was not a concern for me. Also, Matt and I both knew property was less expensive in Klamath Falls, and we could probably afford a home there on a few acres. That thought alone excited us both.

"Let's start looking," I said. And the next weekend, we left the Rogue Valley, drove east up and over the Cascade Mountains, and down into the Klamath Basin. We drove around looking at properties. It was a beautiful area with large ponderosa pine trees scattered along the edge of the basin flats. The Klamath River snaked through the basin, flowing from Klamath Lake west of the small rural city. Klamath Falls is located in a high-desert zone at over four-thousand-foot elevation, the fall weather cool and crisp.

Eleven miles west of Klamath Falls, in a small community called Keno, we found a home we liked on one acre. The house was surrounded by large ponderosa pine trees and overlooked the Klamath River. It was beautiful and we knew we could afford it.

Matt accepted the job offer. We sold our home in Central Point and purchased the scenic Keno home. Again, no mortgage needed. It all happened within two months, and we settled into our new home by Thanksgiving of 2003. We had so much fun that winter, playing in the snow in our own backyard. Matt built a ramp out of snow on the steps of our deck for the boys to sled down. Shasta, our malamute, loved squiggling around in the snow making doggy snow angels.

In the spring of 2004, I was drawing near my four-year date of surviving what doctors considered terminal cancer. Since my diagnosis, Matt and I had grown closer and stronger together. Grant and Clint were seven and five years old.

Cheryl, Clint, Matt and Grant in the Keno house in 2004

We had so much fun living together. For me, our love outweighed any fear of what cancer could bring in the future. I felt so blessed in every way.

As June 27 approached, I got excited about planning a survivorship celebration. Enduring four years of cancer was worth something more than just going out to dinner to acknowledge it. I wanted something special, something big.

One afternoon, I was cruising south on Interstate 5 to my next MRI date at UCSF. Grant and Clint were in the Subaru's back seat. I planned on dropping the boys off at my mom and Pat's house to be spoiled for a few days. The rock group, Journey, played in the stereo as I tapped the wheel with my thumbs to the beat trying to figure a way to celebrate. I wanted something that would make history for me.

I glanced in the rearview mirror at the boys and noticed both of them had their eyes turned to the upper left. My eyes shifted to see what they were fixated on. Oh yeah, Mount Shasta. I should have guessed. I drove past it routinely every few months on my trip to San Francisco.

Mount Shasta

At 14,167-foot elevation, the volcanic mountain loomed on the horizon for more than an hour of the drive. The snow-covered peak was foreboding. Clouds often snagged on the crest. As if the mountain controlled its own weather.

I couldn't help staring at it as I drove by, drawn as if by a magnetic field. I struggled to keep my eyes on the road. If I glanced up, my eyes locked; and I veered over the fog line hitting the wake-up bumps, the loud *bdddddddddddd,* shocking the boys and myself.

"That's it! I'm going to climb to the top of Mount Shasta!" I could see myself at the peak yelling out to the world, "I did it! I beat the odds! I'm alive!"

I saw the sign for Mount Shasta city approaching and pulled off on the highway exit, determined to find the information center. As I drove into downtown, I smiled with excitement. "Why didn't I think of that before?" The boys seemed to think I was crazy talking to myself.

"Where are we going, Mom?" Grant asked. He knew our routine drive from Oregon to California, and we didn't normally swerve off at Mount Shasta city.

"I have to find out how to get to the top of the mountain." He just stared at me. I could tell he was trying to figure out what was going on.

I thought about my "happy home" where I always traveled to during my MRI tests. I often visualized myself at the top of a mountain reaching my arms up to God. It always brought me peace. Climbing to the peak of a real and very large mountain would be momentous. At the top I would reach up to God and thank him.

At the visitors' center we speed-walked to the entrance. Inside, I found a Shasta Mountain Guides brochure and shoved it in my back pocket. I ran out to the car, dragging the boys along behind me. I clipped them into their car seats, and we drove off, my mind reeling with excitement.

Later that day, I sat impatiently in front of my neuro-oncologist, Dr. Chang. She was taking me through a general neurological test that I had on each visit. "Have your eyes follow my finger." She moved her finger from left to right and back. She gave me a big smile. She was always so sweet; I wished I had met her under different circumstances.

"Close your eyes and put one finger to your nose, then the other." I had to laugh because I always felt like I was undergoing a roadside sobriety test, although Dr. Chang was much kinder than any police officer would be. It was hard for me to concentrate on her instructions because I had a question for her.

"Cheryl, please stand up and walk a straight line across the floor, heel to toe." She stood up and moved out of my way, like she thought I would fall and take her out.

Finally I couldn't wait any longer. "Dr. Chang, is there any risk for me being at a high elevation since I've had brain surgery?" I walked slowly, heel to toe, across the room perfectly.

"Not at all," she said.

Her look of curiosity changed to shock when I yelled, "YES! I'm planning to climb Mount Shasta to celebrate my four-year survivorship."

She smiled, patted me on the shoulder. "Have fun."

The plan was sealed. I was going to make the climb. In my mind I was already halfway up. During my drive home, I mentally made a list of things I needed to do. I had four months before June 27, my brain surgery anniversary and the day I wanted to make the climb. To succeed, I needed to start preparing right away.

CHAPTER 11

PREPARING FOR THE CLIMB

When I got home, I greeted Matt with, "How about climbing Mount Shasta?"

He gave me a confused look and a drawn out, "Whaaaat?"

We've always loved hiking together. Some of our best memories were from a backpacking trip to Boulder Lake in the Trinity Alps Wilderness, while we were still in college. Matt spent the mornings fishing for brook trout along the lake's edge, while I lay in the sun on a warm granite boulder, watching him reel them in.

"Are you serious?" Matt questioned.

"YES!" I said, looking at him in anticipation. He had to make the climb with me; it wouldn't be the same without him.

Matt is an outdoor guy, but shuns hard physical activity unless there is a purpose. I was expecting him to say, "And . . . what's the point?" The climb had to end with something he worked for—a deer he hunted, a fish to catch. I could try to convince him there was a mountain goat waiting for him at the peak.

I made my case. "Remember, I've gone deer hunting, turkey hunting, and fishing with you. You owe me!"

"OK, I'll go." He hesitantly agreed, and after a short while of talking about it, he got as excited as I was.

Grant and Clint overheard our discussion. "We want to go too!"

I shook my head. "Mount Shasta's that big mountain we drive by." Their eyes bulged. "Mema and Pappy will probably babysit you guys when we go," I crooned.

"Yeah!" they agreed, feeling they got the better deal. Their grandparents always spoil them with trips to the Dollar Store, dinners at Red Robin, and evenings at the movie theater. The boys ran off to play, and Matt and I sat down to plan the adventure. We had a lot to do.

According to the Shasta Mountain Guides company brochure, only one-third of the climbers make it successfully to the peak. "I can make it!" I said, "Less than 5 percent diagnosed with glioblastoma live for four years. If I can beat those statistics, I can be one of the 33 percent."

We filled out our applications and sent them along with our deposits to the guide service. We received a confirmation of our reservations, a contract to sign, and a long list of rules and regulations. The contract was easy, but we gasped at the long list of gear required.

Soon afterward, we headed to the Ledge, a mountaineering store in Klamath Falls. Good thing we brought a Visa card; it was expensive. At the store we created our own mountain. Its base was formed from lightweight insulated clothing needed to keep us warm in the freezing-cold windy weather: socks, long underwear, gloves, hats, and Windbreaker jackets. The guides' list also required non-cotton underwear. When you sweat during the climb, cotton holds in the moisture against your skin. The cold wetness saps heat from your body. The next layer on our "gear mountain" was cotton-free synthetic underwear for both of us and a cotton-free sports bra for me. Next, we stacked on six water bottles that wouldn't freeze and break in low temperatures. At the peak we balanced sunglasses, ones to block rays reflecting off the snow from burning our eyes. When our mountain of gear was complete, it was actually a beautiful little sight. The multicolored layers looked like natural geological strata in the plateaus of the southwest deserts.

Matt and I also rented some additional equipment needed: mountaineering boots, climbing helmets, ice axes, harnesses, and crampons. We left the store with our arms full.

The next step, equally important, was getting our bodies in shape for the climb. Even though I'd been exercising for years, I hadn't pushed myself enough to reach the athletic level needed to climb the mountain. I was also about twenty pounds overweight.

With only months to get ready, I needed to move quickly. I began exercising hard five days a week. For one hour a day, I either ran outside or worked out on our elliptical machine. I also began lifting weights. My muscles got bigger and my butt got smaller. I lost more than ten pounds! My cardiovascular strength improved too, and I could run faster without getting winded. Each day, when I got off the elliptical, Matt got on and worked out too.

When the day came, we were ready for the climb.

We dropped Grant and Clint off at Mema and Pappy's house and headed to Mount Shasta. We planned to camp overnight in the back of our Ford van at the trailhead. The guides recommended we stay overnight at the seven-thousand-foot elevation to help acclimate our bodies to the lower oxygen level. They said people often failed the climb because of altitude sickness.

We were excited. We couldn't believe the time had finally come. On our way to the trailhead, we stopped at a grocery store in Mount Shasta city and stocked up on food to eat that evening. Our goal was to boost up our carbohydrates to ready our bodies for the climb.

To celebrate, we got a double-decker chocolate cake with chocolate frosting. I'd forbidden myself sugars and sweets over the past four years. I started drooling as we drove up the road to the trailhead. I could smell the sugary cake in the grocery bag and was tempted to grab it out and eat it by myself while Matt drove.

We pulled into the trailhead parking lot by early evening. Matt removed the backseat from our van and set it outside. I rolled out our pads and sleeping bags. Then we both plopped down in the seat beside the van and looked at the peak.

"It's beautiful," I said, trying to imagine myself at the summit.

"Cheryl, look at this!" Matt elbowed my side, and I noticed a sound off to my right.

A young guy had lain down, feet-first, on a long high-speed skateboard and was starting to shoot past us down the paved road. His head was lifted a little so he could look between his feet to see what direction he was going. He leaned to one side or the other to steer.

"That guy is crazy!" Matt said as the guy shot by.

The guy was wearing only shorts, no heavy clothes or gloves to protect him. "I wonder what will happen if his wheel hits a rock," I asked.

Matt and the van at the trailhead

Matt was just shaking his head. "If he falls, he'll get ripped up."

I hated even thinking about it. We had just driven up the steep paved road over ten miles to get to the trailhead. He probably would gain over thirty miles an hour with the gravity pulling him down the slope. Matt and I stared as he disappeared around the corner, tempted to jump in the van and follow him to see what would happen—like a fire truck chaser.

My focus changed quickly when Matt said, "You want the chocolate cake?"

"YES!" I said and jumped into the van, trying to beat him to it.

We crawled into our sleeping bags and lay on our sides, putting the chocolate cake between us. With smiles on our faces and forks in our hands, we tore into it. I can't explain how amazing it tasted. My poor little taste buds had been denied sweets for too long. I closed my eyes and moaned out loud, "Mmmmm," savoring each bite.

Cheryl and the chocolate cake

"You like it, don't you, babe," Matt said in a sexy voice.

People in the car camping next to us probably thought something much more interesting was going on in our van!

We filled up quickly, and then sprawled back on our sleeping bags. "We better go to sleep," Matt said.

I knew it would be hard for us to fall asleep. We were both pumped up with excitement and sugar. "We should try," I said and closed my eyes.

I began thinking about climbing Mount Shasta's *trail*; then my mind turned and wandered to the *trial* of cancer. Both had a need for preparation. Exercising each morning to get physically fit for the climb was like prayer each morning, getting spiritually fit for life's trials. Gathering gear was beneficial for both types of trips: gloves, ice axes, and boots for the mountain; books and Internet Web sites for the cancer.

They're similar. Preparing for a climb up a trail to a mountain peak is like scaling a trial of cancer. Hmmmm. Trails, trials, they're more alike than their spelling.

I closed my eyes and slowly fell asleep. In a dream, I walked slowly up a mountain trail, heading to the peak to talk with God about trials.

CHAPTER 12

GUIDES ARE LIKE GOLD

The next morning, at eight o'clock, we met the guides at Mount Shasta city's outdoor store, The Fifth Season. All of us clients stood around, shuffling our feet, waiting for instructions. Two men approached us. One looked as though in his early forties—short, black-haired, and rugged. The other looked as though in his early twenties—tall and blond. I figured they were our guides.

They stopped abruptly among us, and the older one introduced them, "I'm Genaro, your lead guide, and this is Brandon, my assistant." He looked us over, as if he was trying to figure out who was going to make it to the top and who might make mistakes and put us all at risk.

I eyed him back with a similar inspection. Was he worth trusting to lead me to the summit of Mount Shasta safely? Did I want my harness tied to his? First impressions are always important, and he scored high. It was just the look. I knew you shouldn't judge a book by its cover, but I did. Dressed in high-quality, well-used gear, you could tell he was experienced. He looked confident, in control, and responsible. The way his eyes scanned past each of us gave the impression his brain was moving quickly and calculating a plan.

It was his face that spoke to me and swayed my decision. Genaro, from Mexico, had dark rough skin, like someone who had spent life outdoors. His coal black eyes could go from serious concentration with crow-footed wrinkles at the corners to a deep, open softness within seconds and then back. His eyes told a lot. He seemed to be the type who would risk his life to save another, a person I wanted my harness attached to. If I slipped and fell, he would pull me to safety.

Our guides had already summited Mount Shasta many times that season. It was comforting knowing experienced guides were going to teach us how to use ice axes and crampons and lead our team of eight to the peak of Mount Shasta.

With a pen and checklist in hand, he ordered, "Everyone, dump out your gear on the lawn. I need to look it over." He dug through everyone's gear, not wanting anyone to miss packing what was on the required list or put in unneeded items that would overload the backpack. If he found something he didn't approve, he tossed it off to the side. If he didn't find something required on the list, he'd stand up, point his finger directly to the Outdoor Store, and say, "Go in and get it!" No one argued with him. We knew we weren't leaving until he accepted our gear. After Genaro's final approval, he told us to head out and meet him at the trailhead.

Cheryl – at the trailhead to Mount Shasta

At the trailhead parking lot, our group shuffled around waiting for Genaro and Brandon. Finally we began approaching one another and introducing ourselves, shaking hands in a formal manner, exchanging the standard: names, where you live, what you do.

We all seemed to be in the same age group, the mid-thirties, but we had different backgrounds. There was another husband-and-wife couple, Deborah and David, California police officers. James and Eric were good friends who worked together in computer-type jobs in Southern California. There were two other guys, Mike and John, each on their own. Then Matt and I, another married couple, wildlife biologists.

That was the eight of us, nothing special, just your average folks.

Genaro and Brandon finally arrived, grabbed their gear from the truck's tailgate, and approached us. Genaro said, "All of you go sit on that log near the trailhead." We all followed instructions and sat on the log, looking around, wondering what was up. Again using his deep powerful eyes, Genaro slowly made eye contact with each of us. "Why are you here to climb the mountain? I would like each of you to share what brought you here."

"We'll start," Genaro said. "I'm here because I love climbing to the peak of a mountain. This job lets me teach others how to experience it too. I like that," Genaro said, then turned and looked at Brandon.

"I'm a college student from Colorado studying environmental biology. It's my summer break, and I wanted to earn some money in a fun way," Brandon said.

It got silent for a moment, until someone spoke up. David cleared his throat, then said, "It just seemed like a fun thing to do."

Deborah, his wife, laughed and said, "Not to me! I'd rather be out riding horses, but when it got down to choosing, David won."

We all giggled.

Then James said, "Eric and I made a goal of trying to climb all mountains in California over fourteen-thousand-foot elevation. Last year we climbed Mount Whitney." Eric nodded

Mike and John took their turns then everyone turned and looked at Matt and me.

For some reason I felt nervous. "I've been diagnosed with brain cancer. The doctors gave me less than a year to live. Tomorrow, on June 27, it will be exactly four years since my craniotomy. I wanted to be at the top of Mount Shasta to celebrate and thank God." I stopped there. Everyone stared at me, stunned, like they had questions they wanted to ask, but held off.

Matt sensed I was uncomfortable, knowing I hated being the center of attention. He stood, drawing attention to himself, smiled, and said, "I'm just here to support her, and I'd rather be fishing." Deborah laughed again, as if she could relate to him.

Then Genaro took out his camera and said, "Pack close together, I want a picture."

The group before the climb.
Genaro on the far right with his foot on the log.

In a serious voice he continued, "On average, only one-third of the climbers make it to the top. Brandon is here to take you back down the mountain if you give up." Our eyes all shifted to Brandon. "I will continue to the peak with those who stick with it." The camera clicked. "When it's over and we get back, I will take another picture. It's my goal that all eight of you will be in both photos."

He pointed to the peak and concluded his pep talk, "By tomorrow at noon, we will all be at the top." I took a deep breath and looked at the summit, then focused back on Genaro. I could see he took his job very seriously; it was his personal goal to beat the statistics. We were similar that way. I'd worked hard to beat the cancer survival statistics.

He grabbed his backpack, threw it over his shoulders, and took off up the trail. Our team of eight grabbed our gear, leaped up, and rushed after him, falling into line. Even though it wasn't a normal positive pep talk, it seemed to have encouraged and motivated us. I felt we all respected and trusted Genaro.

I looked at my watch and noted it was about 10:00 AM. We were hiking up to Horse Camp at around eight thousand feet. That afternoon we were to train and practice with ice axes, crampons, and harnesses. After camping that night at Horse Camp, we would leave early the next morning for the final ascent, gaining more than six thousand feet of elevation in only half a day.

Each step up the trail was hard work. The huge plastic mountaineering boots, stiff and heavy, felt like ten pounds of cement on each foot. "These boots suck!" I told Matt, who walked up the trail in front of me, already feeling sore and uncomfortable. "I wish we could hike in our tennis shoes." I heard Matt just make a *hmm* sound in front of me. With not much of a response, I decided to start looking around at the others to keep my mind off my feet.

Most were walking along quietly, glancing around. I think everyone was wondering who would make it to the peak and who would turn back. I was already thinking it would probably be me that failed. I was still a little overweight, and with short legs, I had to take three steps for everyone else's two. Nervous and intimidated, I continued looking around at the others. It seemed they had the same negative thoughts. No one was smiling.

Genaro must have noticed we were discouraged, and he began singing along with every step. I can't remember the words, but I remember it must have been funny because everyone started laughing. Genaro sang partially in Spanish and partially in English. He stopped to the side of the trail occasionally and sang along as we marched by. Smiling, he gave each of us a wink or thumbs-up of encouragement. It must have worked because we sped up and walked with more cheer.

Genaro laughed. "If you pay extra, I'll sing more. Maybe, say, fifty dollars for each song in English, and you can get a good deal for Spanish, only a dollar fifty." We all laughed. Genaro ran back to the front of the group, and even though none of us agreed to his deal, he continued singing along with each step. I loved it.

As I hiked, my mind went off to cancer as it often did each day. During that climb, I would have crumbled if wise mentors hadn't walked alongside me as a guide.

Cheryl and her mom Judy

Mom, my primary mentor, had always been there from day one since I was diagnosed. If my mind began to fall into a crevasse, she would pull me out and encourage me on. She never told me what to do, just opened the door so I could see. She never made me feel weak, as though I needed her to succeed, but lifted me up to see my own strength. Not waiting for me to seek her out, she just appeared in my life when needed. One day I would receive a card in the mail with a Bible verse for encouragement. Sometimes she would send a book or an article torn from a magazine. Another day the phone would ring. I'd pick it up to hear, "Hello, just calling to say hi." She would give me words of wisdom or would just listen as my emotions poured out.

On the Internet, I met long-term brain cancer survivors who became my mentors. They answered questions about what to expect and how to handle it. They'd already been through the trials of brain surgery, radiation, chemotherapy, and all the pain that comes along with them. They gave me advice on how to maneuver around the unsuspected slick patches of possible icy avalanche snow.

I met one long-term glioblastoma survivor, Matthew Fullerton, who faithfully e-mailed back anytime I wrote to him with tons of questions. The main thing I remembered was his positive attitude of encouragement and the way he always signed with "KOKO—Keep On Keeping On!" That is exactly what I needed to hear because all along, survival statistics gave me the impression there was no way to keep on going.

I was also blessed with two wise mentors from church, Wanda and Zelia. They were mature veterans who found me during my war on cancer. They were already seasoned and had endured years of trials. I spent hours with each of them on an old wood swing in the backyard or sitting at a kitchen table with hot cups of Earl Grey tea. I listened to their wisdom. They were humble and gentle, even though they were more sensible than most around them. Just being near them, their knowledge seeped from them to me as if by osmosis. With their help, I gained wisdom about life and living well, way beyond what I could have learned on my own.

Ascending Mount Shasta, I realized I would always need mentors and guides no matter what climb I was making. They were more valuable than gold, and I would travel through life always holding on tightly to that treasure.

Lost in thought, I almost tripped and fell when Matt stopped in front of me. I looked up and saw we were already at Horse Camp. I felt relieved we had made it to the first landmark. Thank goodness we had guides. I looked at the peak, with faith that I would make it.

CHAPTER 13

STEP-BY-STEP

Sierra Club's historic Horse Camp building

We arrived at Horse Camp at noon. Our group had hiked two hours, and we were hungry. Breaking out our sandwiches and water, we leaned against the U.S. Forest Service historic building and began to eat lunch and enjoy the beautiful view.

Natural colors filled the scene, like an artist's painting. Light blues crossed the sky. Varying shades of white snow molded its way through sharp points and horizontal slope edges. Scattered grays, blacks, and reds, in varying sized rocks, patched here and there through the blanket of snow. Changing greens and browns of

97

coniferous trees wove along the bottom of the landscape view. The building we leaned on was built with large boulders, cool and smooth against my back. Nature presented the beauty better than any artist could capture.

Horse Camp, at eight-thousand-foot elevation, is near the top of the tree zone. Short and squat Shasta red firs and mountain hemlocks dot the area. Not too far up past camp, trees thin out, and only rocks and snow cover the ground. The sun was out. Even in near-freezing temperatures, the rays warmed my cheeks. I sat back and relaxed, munching on my sandwich, enjoying the peace. Our night at Horse Camp would get our bodies more acclimated to the elevation.

Tents at Horse Camp

After the last crumb of lunch was gone, Genaro led us to where we were to set up the tents for the night. Breaking us into groups of two, he instructed, "Dig the snow to make flat spots where you'll set up your tent." I was glad Matt was my partner because he did most of the digging and tent building; I mostly smiled sweetly at him.

We did work together pounding stakes into the ice around the tent to hold the tent base firm to the ground in case of heavy winds. By mid-afternoon, a handful of blue tents were up and ready for that evening. Genaro gathered us and said, "Get your gear. We're heading out for practice."

Soon, ice axes in hand, crampons attached to boots, and harnesses clipped to our bodies, we were ready to go. We hiked about twenty minutes from camp to a steep, icy hillside, and Genaro told us, "We're going to practice with your mountaineering gear and learn to work as a team."

I was excited about this. I wanted to prepare before tackling the real thing. Without practice, it would be like an inexperienced greenhorn jumping on a horse to take a ride, only to be bucked off within seconds. I didn't want to be bucked off Mount Shasta.

While standing on a steep slope, Genaro said, "Let's start with the ax. I want you to fall and purposely slide down the slope, then try stopping yourselves. When you begin to slide, roll over to your stomach, digging your ax at shoulder level into the ice, and then kicking each crampon into the slope. Count one, two, three as you do it. If you slam your crampons and ax hard enough into the ice, it will stop your fall. It's called, self-arrest."

"If you don't self-arrest"—he smiled, turned, and pointed to the bottom—"you'll end up down there." The sparkle in his eye told me he hoped someone would slide to the bottom of the little practice slope, just to get a good laugh.

We all smiled. No one was very nervous because the incline descended only fifty feet before it leveled out. If we couldn't stop ourselves with the ice axes, we might be embarrassed, but wouldn't slide off into a crevasse.

Allowing ourselves to slide was not a problem. The ice was slick. It wasn't puffy white snowflakes that make good snow angels; it was like hard grayish pavement.

Stopping ourselves was harder than it sounded. Each one of us, one time or another, slid out of control. Some slipped only a few feet, while others went wild for more than twenty before they stopped themselves with the ax. There was a lot of hooting and hollering—"ahhh," "stop," "yoo-hoo"—and good-natured ribbing. It was fun. Some people let themselves slide to the bottom just for the fun of it. We all laughed a lot. I was able to stop myself quickly

Cheryl with her ice ax

when practicing. I hoped it would be that easy if I really needed to do it. After an hour, we had the technique down.

"OK, let's move to the next step," Genaro said. "We're going to work with our harnesses." We could see the seriousness in Genaro's eyes. The fun time was over. "When we get on to extremely dangerous slopes or near crevasses, we will break into groups and tie ourselves together." Looking at each of us, he warned, "There are times when an ice ax may not stop you." At that, we all became as serious as he was. He reminded us that people had died on that mountain.

"If a person on your rope team slips and falls, the others will instantly fall and self-arrest." Jerking on the rope attached to his harness, Genaro continued, "Since you're tied together tightly, you should be able to stop the one who's sliding."

We all looked around at one another. Who was I going to be tied to? Would I trust them to save my life?

Genaro pointed around. "You, you, and you will be together." He turned, looked at me, and said, "You will be with me." I felt relieved. I knew he wanted me attached to him because I

100

was the weakest smallest one, fighting cancer. I didn't feel insulted, just appreciative. "You too," he said pointing to Matt.

I was linked with harness and rope between Genaro in front of me and Matt behind. I felt very comfortable between the two of them, in the best and safest spot. I had scored.

After three hours of practice, we went back to camp and crashed out. The guides cooked us pasta and lentil soup for dinner. We ate quietly, mentally going through each step we would take the next day.

Dinner could have been cardboard for all I cared. I just wanted to go to sleep so I could wake up the next morning ready to climb. We only had four hours until wake-up time. Matt and I went to the tent and crawled deep into our sleeping bags. I'd never slept on snow before; it was freezing despite the high-quality insulating pad between me and the ice.

"Are you comfortable?" Matt asked.

There was a quiet pause. "No," I said. "Are you?"

"No." Silence. Then Matt asked, "Are you warm?"

Another pause. "No, how about you?" I asked.

A slight movement from Matt. "Hmm, not really."

Mummy bags have that name for a reason. That was it with our conversation.

I closed my eyes and tried to doze off, but deep sleep never came. I couldn't help but remember the months I'd spent in my mummy bag one summer break in college.

I'd worked as a wilderness patrol for the Shasta-Trinity National Forest. My job was to help backpackers, who had been hurt or lost in the wilderness, and also to clean up and carry out any garbage hikers left behind. I would generally enter the wilderness with a thirty-pound backpack, but would often leave carrying an extra hefty ten pounds of garbage. Good thing the way back to the trailhead was downhill.

Usually during the weekdays, the other backpackers were gone, and I was there alone. One night, sleeping near a stream, I had a horrible nightmare. It only happened once, but I never got it out of my memory. In the dream, someone sneaked up on me while I was asleep and pulled the drawstring on the face hole of my mummy bag. Tightly closed, I was completely sealed in the bag, head and all.

Then I was dragged into the cold stream water, and my sealed head was pushed underwater. They were trying to drown me. I was trapped in the mummy bag.

I woke up panicked, my heart pounding. Each time I fell back asleep that night, the dream repeated itself.

Ever since then, sleeping deep in a mummy bag was about impossible for me. It wasn't even worth trying. On top of that, I had to pee so bad I couldn't even move. But I didn't want to crawl out of my sleeping bag and freeze my butt off making yellow snow. I pinched my thighs together, tighter, and waited out the night.

The guides woke us up at midnight. We had two hours to eat and get our gear on. Genaro heated up water on a camp stove, so we could make instant oatmeal and hot chocolate. Most of us were too anxious about the climb to eat much of anything. Genaro must have noticed we weren't eating. "Make sure you get enough to drink and eat today. You'll need it. Also, at high elevations you can get headaches. If you do, let me know." I picked up some hot chocolate and oatmeal.

To make sure I wouldn't freeze, I layered my clothes—five layers on my torso; three on my legs; and two on my hands, feet, and head. The heavy and awkward confining clothes made me feel and look like the Michelin tire man. With the loaded daypack, heavy mountaineering boots, helmet, and an ice ax in my left hand, I could barely move. If I did fall, I would be like a turtle stuck on its back.

How was I ever going to go pee on a steep icy slope if needed? Maybe I could hold it in all day long. I was getting the jitters and my stomach started to hurt.

It was still pitch-black when we headed out at 2:00 AM. We wore our headlamps to light the way. Mine only lit a few feet in front of me. Everything else was pitch- black, except far away up the slope I could see the lights of other climbers. People who'd camped at Lake Helen had started out further upslope that morning. Their lamps flashed as they occasionally turned their heads downhill toward us. They looked like strings of blinking Christmas lights.

The icy slope was so slick I had to kick my sharp metal crampons into the ice to hold in place with each step. Keeping my footing took a lot of concentration and effort. Early on, I began getting tired, and my legs began to burn. The sun hadn't risen, and I couldn't see the mountaintop, but I knew it was still a long way off.

I had to set a goal to keep myself motivated and moving. I looked down at my watch and thought about a time target. Just the thought of climbing for ten minutes was too much. I decided the aim of taking one step at a time was my limit. How embarrassing. I started to cry. I was glad it was still dark outside so the others, focusing on their feet, couldn't see my tears.

Genaro knew we were already getting tired. "Don't try to hike too fast," he said. "Take a slow pace, called the 'rest step,' so you won't get worn-out too soon."

With each step, I started counting in my mind, *One, two. One, two. One, two.* I could see why soldiers chant cadences over and over when they march. I couldn't think about continuing for miles, just one step at a time. I figured Genaro purposely started us out in the darkness so we couldn't see the peak, only our feet one step ahead with our headlamps. *One, two. One, two.* I continued and my mind wandered back to cancer.

My perilous climb through brain cancer took one day at a time. If I had looked ahead, the peak would have appeared impossible. It's like the parable about eating an elephant: "It is doable, if you take one bite at a time." If you try to grab the whole elephant all at once, it would fall on top of you. Squish, you're gone.

Every time I started to see the big picture of brain cancer, I had to stop and narrow it down. Based on what most glioblastoma patients go through, I knew the climb would be hard. The tumors and treatments often caused disabilities like loss of speech, sight, movement, and cognitive abilities; also seizures, headaches, and changes in personality. Toward the peak, glioblastomas grow uncontrollably, taking over all the space in the skull, squishing the good cells to nothingness. The forlorn trails through brain cancer never are an easy path.

When first diagnosed, I met three other people with glioblastoma, and we became supportive friends. One by one they passed away. Over the years, I've made and lost many friends to brain cancer. I can't even count them on my fingers and toes; it feels more like the numbers of the hairs on my head.

Looking ahead at the peak, I saw my own probable suffering. Beyond, I saw pain my family would endure. Would Matt lie sleepless on the couch because he couldn't bear being alone in our bed? Would Clint cry himself to sleep at night holding his teddy bear because I wasn't there to tuck him in? Would Grant fall, cut his knee and cry, and not have me there to comfort him? Would my two little boys remember me as a happy, loving mom or someone in a hospital bed, sick and dying?

During my climb through cancer, there was only one thing that helped me live in the moment and focus on one step at a time, only one thing that kept me from looking ahead at the intimidating peak looming in the darkness. It was my own spiritual headlamp; my Lord, Jesus Christ.

Continuing up Mount Shasta, kicking my crampons into the ice, I thought about my spiritual lamp. All I had to do was look into Christ's light with each step I took. That way, there was a peaceful glow in it. I was reminded of a children's song I learned long ago in Sunday school, but heard it a new way.

This little light of mine, I'm going to let it shine
This little light of mine, I'm going to let it shine,
let it shine, let it shine, let it shine
Hide it under a bush oh no, I'm going to let it shine
Hide it under a bush oh no, I'm going to let it shine,
let it shine, let it shine, let it shine

I smiled and started quietly singing my Sunday school song to myself as I continued to climb up Mount Shasta—one step at a time.

CHAPTER 14

OVERCOMING ANXIETY

Not too far into the climb, I started getting nauseous. High elevation can cause headaches and nausea, but we were only at about nine thousand feet.

We stopped for a break at a large rock outcrop poking up through the snow and ice. Everybody settled down, and my stomach did a flip-flop. I felt like I was going to throw up and mess my pants at the same time. No one else looked sick. I panicked and tried to figure out where I could hide and let it all out. It was still early in the morning and pitch-black. The only place I could hide was on the backside of the huge rock everyone was sitting on.

I sneaked off around the rock as fast as I could, trying not to draw any attention to myself. I rapidly threw off my backpack and searched for my poop bag. For sanitary reasons, the U.S. Forest Service gave each of us a special bag for defecation. After filling the bag, we were to seal it up and pack it back down the mountain to deposit it in a special garbage can at the trailhead. If you got caught going number two on the pure white snow, you would be fined over $500.

I wasn't sure I could avoid breaking the law. The pressure was like a shaken soda can ready to explode. I ripped down my three layers of clothes as fast as I could. Out it came. I hoped I hit the target and not my boots. While holding the poop bag in place and balancing on the slick ice, I tried to lean forward as far as I could. Vomit felt like it was going to eject out the other end. All I could think was, *Where's my toilet paper?*

I was so relieved that I'd hit the target, found the toilet paper, and gulped back the bile that crawled up my throat. Sealing the bag up, I hid it in my backpack, hoping it wouldn't leak. How gross! I sneaked back around the rock to the group, hoping no one knew what had happened. I was too humiliated to even tell Matt about it. My stomach still hurt. I kept taking big deep breaths and sips of water, hoping to calm the nausea.

As soon as we started climbing again, I felt fine. *What's up with this? How can I go from feeling so bad to feeling good that fast?* We climbed a while longer making it to our next stop at Lake Helen. It was light outside by then, and we could look around and see the scenery. Lake Helen was not really a lake, but a large flat spot up the mountain at about ten thousand feet. There were more than twenty tents set up around the rim of the flats.

As soon as we stopped, my nausea and diarrhea returned. *Oh no! The Forest Service only gave me one bag! I've already filled it up! What am I going to do?* I turned to Matt with pleading eyes and whispered, "Matt, I need your poop bag now!" Seeing my desperation, he dug into his backpack and pulled out his bag as fast as he could.

I grabbed it, panicked, and looked around. There was no place to hide. I took off toward the tents as fast as I could, hoping to find one to squat behind out of sight. However with each step, or waddle I should say, I felt like I wasn't going to make it.

As soon as I got behind the first tent out of sight of my team, I ripped down my pants. It was then that I looked up the steep slope above Lake Helen and noticed numerous climbers that could look right back down at me. At that point, I didn't care. What else could I do, but cry and laugh at the same time?

When I got back to the group, Matt pulled me aside and asked, "Is everything OK?"

I tried to not cry again and said, "I'm so sick and hope I won't need a third bag." The group started to put on their backpacks, ready to move out again.

Matt gave me a quick hug and asked, "Do you want to keep going?" I nodded, and we turned to follow the others.

Once we started moving again, my stomach felt better. I finally realized what was going on. When moving, my mind focused on taking the next step. When I stopped, I started thinking about the negatives.

During the stops, my mind would wander. *How much longer will this take?* I'd look down at my watch. I'd massage my legs. *With this pain, will they make it to the top?* I shivered. *I'm freezing.*

I remembered back to what I learned at the WINGS seminar. "You are what you think you are. You have to put mind over matter to overcome it." It was my anxious thoughts that made me sick, not the elevation. I was sure of it. I was doing it to myself!

I had noticed the same problem with nausea and diarrhea during my climb through cancer. When I was first diagnosed, I often sat inactive in hospital beds with nothing else to do but sit and think. Unfortunately, my thoughts were often negative.

One time, scheduled for surgery, I worried about all the "what-ifs." What if I come out of surgery unable to talk? What if I am paralyzed on the right side of my body? What if I lose my memory and don't recognize Matt or the boys? That's when my stomach gurgled, and I got nauseous. I ran to the nearest restroom. Thank goodness for hospital gowns. I'd never appreciated their style before. But I finally realized the special design, the open slit up the back, was made for easy rear-end access during toilet sprints.

While fighting cancer, I often got another type of sickness when my mind wandered off to the negative. It wasn't the same as nausea but, in many ways, way worse.

Depression.

It could take over, leaving me with an empty feeling in my heart, a doomsday, the sky-is-falling feeling. On a day like that, I could be at Disneyland or be the winner of the million-dollar Publishers Clearing House Sweepstakes and still feel life was no good.

I don't always know what set me off, but I do know where my thoughts went. *Poor, pitiful me. Why me? Why can't anyone understand what I am going through? I'm all alone.* While in the me, me, me zone, it felt like a big hurricane wave was washing me away into an ocean of gloom. It was hard to swim out of it too because I could justify it. *I have the right to feel this way. I have cancer and the doctors tell me I will die.*

If I kept active, my anxiety and depression reduced. Cleaning house, doing laundry, cooking dinner, playing games with the boys, running, biking—anything that kept me moving was good. But sometimes I couldn't keep myself busy and active. Like when I was lying in bed trying to fall asleep, or driving. Finally, I would remember an even better way to fix my slump, and I'd say to myself. *Why didn't I think of this hours ago?* Turning my thoughts to God.

One night, a few days before my scheduled MRI, I was lying in bed alone, trying to go to sleep. I couldn't. My mind kept living through bad news the neuron-oncologist could give me about the MRI results. *The tumor is back, the size of a lemon, you need brain surgery again.* I began to cry my pillow wet with tears. I tried to weep quietly so Matt, in the other room watching TV, couldn't hear me. It got hard to breathe. It felt like a heavy weight was pushing down on my chest. My body felt like it turned to stone and couldn't move.

At that point, I reached out to God. "I need you, God. I wish you could be here and hold me tight in your arms," I whispered. Within seconds things changed. I'm still amazed to this day at the miracle of it. It started with a tingling all over my body. Then warmth covered me from head to toe. I felt a gentle pressure on every cell of my body, like I was being hugged deep inside. I began to cry even more, at that point, tears of joy. It's like God touched me, hugged me, and gave me peace. I took a big deep breath, relaxed, and fell asleep. I wish I could bottle that amazing feeling. Take it out and drink it in, every day.   The good news is: that's not needed. It's available all the time. It just depends on where I focus my thoughts.

As I continued climbing up Mount Shasta, I was so happy to have realized what caused my nausea and diarrhea. All I had to do was change my thoughts, and I could overcome the sickness. My stomach felt fine the rest of the climb. I didn't need to find a third bag.

CHAPTER 15

HOLD ON TO YOUR HEART

*The Heart (center) Climbers can be seen as dark specks making
their way up to the base of The Heart.*

By mid-June, much of the fluffy winter snow had melted off
Mount Shasta's southern aspect.   Dense ice and large scattered
glaciers remained.   Not far above Lake Helen, we began to
switchback up the slope on the right side of what is known as The
Heart—a huge heart-shaped patch of rock surrounded by icy snow.
It's large enough to be seen from miles away on the highway below.

Once climbers pass The Heart, the most difficult part of the climb begins—the Red Banks and Misery Hill. Most climbers are already worn-out after climbing through what is considered the easiest part.

At The Heart, many climbers lose their own, turn around, and head back down. Like the Tin Woodsman in *The Wizard of Oz*, without a heart, you lose faith and doubt can get the best of you. If the Tin Man didn't keep working hard to find a heart, he never would have found one. He never would have made it to his personal mountain peak.

It was at the bottom of The Heart that Mike turned around and headed back down. I was surprised. If anyone failed, I didn't think it would be him. He had new expensive mountaineering gear and appeared to be in good physical shape. His facial expression and posture spoke to us all. He had lost his heart. We stood and watched as he joined up with another guide and group of climbers that were heading down. Brandon was able to stay with our remaining team of eight minus one.

I'd figured if anyone failed, it would have been me. I was the one who had gotten nauseous and filled up two poop bags. I was shorter, smaller, and physically weaker than everyone else on the team. As we watched Mike walk away, I'm sure we all wondered who might be the next one to lose heart.

I remembered Genaro telling us, "It's mind over matter." He felt accomplishing the climb was 80 percent mental attitude and 20 percent physical fitness. Intrigued, I started watching the climbers that passed by me on their way back down the mountain.

Some hikers, heads drooping, making no eye contact with other people, passed by with defeated looks on their faces. I'm pretty sure they were the ones who didn't make it to the peak. Had they lost their heart, lost their faith, and given up?

The spirit of climbers who succeeded was obvious and so different. They strutted past, faces lit with pride. With happy eyes, glowing, and big smiles, they looked directly at others walking by and said, "You can make it!" "You're almost there, keep going. Don't give up!" "You've got to see it, you'll love the peak!" They still had their hearts beating with joy.

We took a break. I looked up at the jagged rocky Red Banks. It was nothing but intimidating—blood-red rocks shaped like sharp deadly knives. My chest started pounding like my heart was trying to escape. Putting my hand over my chest, I held on tight. I wasn't going to lose it. I wasn't going to fail.

Just like the little red train engine in the children's book I'd read many times. *I think I can, I think I can, I think I can. Heading down is not an option.* I argued with myself. I was reminded of the same doubt I'd suffered during my climb through cancer.

On the BRAINTMR e-mail list, I'd met hundreds of wonderful people who are also battling brain tumors. Daily, we e-mailed back and forth, comparing experiences and encouraging one another. Almost weekly, I climbed my own personal Misery Hill when I got the news that someone on the list had died. My heart ached, like sorrow was trying to rip it out. *Why am I still alive, if they're not? They had stronger and braver souls than me.* I would cry to myself.

When I got bad news, I would stoop over and grasp my chest. I struggled to breathe and it felt like my heart is trying to climb up out my throat. Gagging and coughing, I swallowed it back down. So far I've never lost it.

I know my friends who'd passed away hadn't failed and lost their heart. They fought to the end with a strong spirit. Maybe it was just time. I learned from families on the BRAINTMR list how my friends often pass away in peace, with glowing eyes and a smile. They hadn't lost their heart. On the list it was announced, "They gained their wings."

They didn't have to climb to the peak with their own two feet. In faith, with their hearts, they got wings to fly. They are angels at the top of life's mountains, watching us from above, encouraging us.

Determined to make it to the top of Mount Shasta, I held tight to my heart. As long as I kept my faith, I knew God would give me the strength. Just knowing that gave me the attitude Genaro said I needed to keep going. I glanced at the Red Banks and felt the warm sun shining on my cheek. I knew angels were at the top waiting for me. I could hear them calling. My hand relaxed and slid down from my heart to my side. I knew I could make it. God may not always give me the strength to make it to the peak on my own two feet, but if needed, he will always give me the wings. I continued the climb.

CHAPTER 16

TEAMWORK

Our remaining team—seven climbers and two guides—continued to ascend Mount Shasta. My initial attitude about climbing with a group of strangers had been negative. For me it was a personal experience. Initially, I would rather have done it alone with only God and Matt. I always tried to be self-sufficient, rarely asking for help. I accepted the fact I needed a guide, but I didn't want to be surrounded by a team of strangers. Not too far into the climb, that notion changed.

As we climbed up past the Heart, the slope got extremely steep. I felt like I was trying to hold on to a vertical ice wall. The only way to keep myself from sliding down the slope was to kick my crampons hard into the ice with each step, while swinging the ax into the wall at shoulder level.

Kick, kick, pick. Kick, kick, pick. With each step, I hoped I wouldn't break loose from the ice. The risk of uncontrollably sliding hundreds of feet down the mountain was worrisome. In a fall like that, most likely, the crampons or ax would end up stuck in my thigh instead of the ice. Not a fun thought.

Genaro stopped, turned, and called out, "Time to tie up." We stopped, and Genaro passed down the rope for each of us to attach at waist level. The metallic click of the carabineers snapping into place, securing us to the rope, comforted me.

Genaro broke us into two groups, one of four and the other of five. We tied ourselves together about eight feet apart. It was important to keep that distance so if someone fell, they would not slam into the person behind. I was in the group of four. Genaro was in front of me, Matt behind me, and John behind him. Once we were all attached, we began to climb again.

It was at that point I really began to appreciate being part of a team. I felt safer and supported. Even though we never made eye contact or talked to one another during that part of the climb (we were too busy concentrating on our footing), just being connected to others was comforting. They could become my lifesavers. The rope that tied us together could end up being as important as my umbilical cord had been.

The team roped together

As we continued to climb, I noticed other benefits of teamwork. While roped to the others, I had to keep a steady pace. If I stopped, it could tug the person ahead of me and pull them over. Even if I wanted to pause and rest, I had to keep going at a quicker steady pace than I would have done alone. We stopped as a team only when Genaro called out, "Break."

As I kicked and picked my way up the slope, my mind wandered to memories of teams while climbing my life's mountains. After my diagnosis, many supportive team members surrounded me. They were tied to me by spirit, ready to grab me if I fell.

My Community Bible Church family was like a football team. I was the one running with the cancer ball, but they surrounded me with offense and defense. It often felt like I didn't actually run the field. The offense picked me up and carried me.

While undergoing radiation, church members brought our family a dinner each day, assuming I would be too tired to cook one myself. If I was too fatigued and needed an afternoon nap, I could drop Grant off at our church's preschool—for free. Most days I got a card in the mail from someone at church with loving and encouraging handwritten words, even from people I'd never met in person. I filled up a shoebox with cards, each one much more touching and supportive than any Hallmark card could be.

The defense line was there for me too. It felt like huge strong linebackers surrounded, ready to tackle anything that threatened me. I remember late one night we saw headlights pulling into our long gravel driveway, when we still lived in the forestland house twenty minutes from town. We wondered who would be out there in the middle of the night. A van pulled up and parked at the bottom of the steps leading up to our sliding glass door. At that time of night, I was already in my PJs and Matt in his underwear. We sneaked to the window and peaked out.

We could see that the huge van was filled with numerous people, but it was too dark to identify them. Time went by and the van just sat there. Matt and I were trying to decide what to do.

"Who do you think they are?" I asked Matt.

"I guess I'd better get dressed and go down there," Matt responded. Not really wanting to deal with it, we waited another five minutes hoping they would drive off.

"Maybe someone's lost?" I said.

"I'd better go see," Matt moaned. We both grabbed our clothes and got dressed.

Good thing we did because as we approached the sliding glass door, we were shocked to see two teens sprinting up the steps. They would have been embarrassed and shocked too if they'd seen Matt standing there in his underwear.

With huge smiles on their faces, they taped a note to the door, turned, and ran off. We recognized the teens from church and started laughing. Matt opened the door and grabbed the note. It said "You've been the subject of a drive-by praying."

Matt and I collapsed on the couch, able to breath easy again. Our hearts were touched and comforted knowing a team of teenagers loved us enough to drive twenty minutes out of town to our home to pray for us at our doorstep. Even though these young ones were much smaller than a defensive line on a professional football team, their protection felt much stronger.

Genaro called out, "Break." And it brought me back to the present. I stopped and looked around at Matt and the others I was roped to. I smiled at each of them. Climbing Mount Shasta, I gained a new appreciation for being part of a team.

CHAPTER 17

THROUGH THE PAIN

Climbers traverse the Red Banks

We got to the top of the Heart and unhooked our harnesses. Next came the Red Banks. Snow free, we could see the steep route through blood-colored rocks and gravel. It felt good to be off the ice, but the rocks didn't look any easier. After a short break, we continued the climb.

Each step was like climbing extra-tall stairs. It felt like my knee might hit the bottom of my chin as gravity pressed my weight down. I struggled to push myself up. My thighs began to burn. If I paused to take a deep breath, my legs shook and felt like they were going to collapse. I thought my legs would go on strike, and I would be stuck in one place.

Genaro must have noticed. "Keep moving. If you stop when your legs are in pain, it will cause your muscles to tighten up, and it will get worse. If you want to make it to the peak, keep going and work through your pain."

I tried to take my thoughts away from my agonizing thighs. *What else can I think about?* Unfortunately, my mind quickly turned and refocused on pain elsewhere. My shins cried that they were torture victims too.

The stiff, hard, mountaineering boots I had rented ground into the front of my shins with every step. They must have not been broken in well. It felt like a saw was cutting into my shinbone and applying pressure to snap it in two, sending a shock of pain racing up my leg into my upper body. I started to walk sort of sideways to take the pressure off the front of my shins. Tears started to pour and run down my cheeks. I didn't want anyone to see, but I couldn't hold them back.

Genaro must have seen me walking funny and called out, "Break." He pointed to me and then to a rock. "Come over here and sit down. Let me take a look at your boots."

I sat down and pulled my pant legs up and pushed down my socks to take a look at my shins. Just touching them shot pain up past my knee. Some of the skin had already been torn, and bruises were forming.

Genaro shook his head, but didn't say anything. He unlaced my boots, loosening the tops. He then re-shifted each boot, moving it back and forth and pushing my heel down, trying to reduce the pressure. "Stand up and try that out. What do you think?" Genaro asked.

It didn't help much. I forced out a smile and replied, "It's OK. Thanks." I hoped he didn't notice the quivering in my voice.

When we started to climb again, I was overwhelmed with agony in my thighs and shins! What was I going to do? I had to keep going. If I kept thinking about the pain, I knew I would become immobile. I tried to refocus my thoughts and decided to reflect on other pains in the past that had been worse. *I've felt worse than this! Just thinking about it will make this pain not feel so bad!*

It took a little while to come up with one because on a scale of one to ten, I was close to ten!

After my craniotomy, the pain in my head ranked up there too. Dr. Delashaw had cut a hole in my skull, taken out the tumor, and then screwed the bone back together with titanium straps. Six screws and over fifteen stitches later, my head was back together (as good as it could be).

My doctors had prescribed some good meds to fight the pain. But I'm the type of person who thinks, *I don't need no stinkin' drugs!* Just standing there wasn't so bad, but any movement or anything touching my head brought serious pain. No one could even breathe on the left side of my head. At night, in order to sleep, I had to cup my hands over the craniotomy area so the pressure of my super soft pillow wouldn't touch it.

OK, that was bad, but my legs hurt way worse! Oh yeah, when my brain was hemorrhaging, before my surgery, that was a ten plus! No, I can't let my thoughts go there. That pain was too traumatic, too bad to even think about. I might throw up.

OK, think, think, think. My mind went on and on. Labor, yah, labor. Now that was painful!

During my first labor, Grant got stuck in my birth canal. His arm was twisted up around his neck, so he couldn't fit through. I had been pushing for over two hours and was worn-out. It felt like a locomotive trying to rip through my body. I had been cut deep, down there, to make more space for Grant to fit through, but it didn't help.

The doctor was determined to not do a caesarian, so she called out for forceps. They looked like huge salad spoons. No lie, they were bigger than the size of my hands.

Shoving the forceps in, she grabbed Grant's head, then attached a vacuum to his scalp and pulled as hard as she could with both. I was worried she was going to pop Grant's head off! The doctor yelled, "Super abdominal pressure!" And a nurse jumped up on a stool next to the bed. She placed both hands on my upper belly, with her elbows locked straight, and pushed as hard as she could, bearing down with all her weight—like pushing toothpaste out of the tube. She pushed from one end, while the doctor pulled from the other. I can't even describe the pain. I felt like I was having an out-of-body experience in order to escape from the agony.

Yes, that experience won the contest and gets the highest pain prize. But wait, it got worse, an emotional pain that came from deep within, an anguish that afflicted every cell in my body.

When Grant was finally pulled out, he was pale and limp. They massaged him and tried to stimulate his breath, but he didn't respond. His legs drooped and he was perfectly still. They sucked the mucous out of his throat, and there was still no breathing. I was so worn-out it felt like I was floating out of my body above the room observing what was happening.

Death. Don't even think about it. Death.

That kind of pain is off the scale. It's up in the millions. Just thinking about it as I climbed Mount Shasta gave me an epidural to my spine, unconsciously taking away the pain from my legs.

My mind went on to more emotional anguish. It was like I was traveling in the waters of a raging river, caught in class-4 rapids, approaching a waterfall. My thoughts went back to death again, this time about mine. I hate when my mind goes there. Even though I try to hide from the thought, it creeps in. It's ugly. It's indescribable. I feel like I am going to implode.

Grant successfully made it through his birth and, today, is a healthy little boy. But what if I died? Just the thought of my boys' life without me was unbearable. Not being there when they need me. Them calling out my name needing me as all children need their moms. Shackled to death—unable to get to them, hold them, and comfort them. Not able to see them evolve and grow into young men. Not being there to congratulate them when they graduate from school. Not being at their weddings.

Sometimes, in thought, I already feel like I am dead. My mind sees the world without me. I see Matt sitting on the couch, each arm wrapped around the boys, all of them in tears.

There is another thought that crumbles me. What if I died and Grant and Clint didn't remember me? What if Matt got remarried and they considered her their mom? Will they call her mom? It's a selfish pain, but it hurts. It really hurts. Yes, emotional pain causes more suffering than physical pain.

Grant, Clint, Matt and our dog Tule

As I continued my climb up Mount Shasta, I realized the importance of working through the pain whether it was physical or emotional. If I wanted to get to the peak, cross the finish line, or hit my goal, I had to keep going. Athletes have gone through pain in sports to win. Soldiers have gone through pain in wars to defend their country. Mothers have gone through the pain of labor to hold their cherished little ones. There's pain in life. And to get to the other side, it takes work.

Working through pain builds strength and perseverance. Bones that break end up stronger in the broken area after they've healed.

All of these thoughts reeled through my mind as I climbed up the mountain. *Just like during child delivery, take big deep breaths and work through the pain,* I thought to myself. Thank goodness, my mind finally landed on what always gives me the strength to work though anything: God.

Why didn't I think about God to begin with! The physical pain didn't lessen much, but at least, I knew God would give me strength to keep going. I knew one day I would look back and think the agony was worth it. Like during Grant's birth, pain faded away when I held him in my arms.

CHAPTER 18

TAKING A BREAK

We finally made it to the top of Red Banks. Genaro, realizing we were all exhausted, called out, "Break." I slid my daypack off and looked around for Matt. He had already put his pack under his head as a pillow, curled up on the ground, and was deep asleep. Matt sleeps hard and could snore through an earthquake. I found a rock nearby and slowly lowered myself down to its hard surface, trying not to aggravate the pain in my legs.

Matt asleep during a break

TAKING A BREAK

I couldn't let myself fall asleep like Matt. I knew if I lay down, I wouldn't get back up. Matt was definitely blessed with the ability to fall asleep quickly, then within seconds, wake up again, ready to go. He could jump up and hike like he never stopped. I wish I could do that. I just sat there and stared at him.

Genaro called out to everyone, "Remember to breathe deeply during your breaks."

It was easy for me to forget about the significance of breathing deep while climbing because I would get hung up on the pain, the coldness, and the difficulty of climbing up a steep mountain. So I was glad when Genaro would stop us for a break and remind us to breathe.

Sitting up straighter gave my lungs more capacity. We were at about 12,500-foot elevation; and the higher you get, the thinner the air is. With less oxygen, it was important to consciously breathe deep so we wouldn't get depleted.

I took a big breath, inhaling cold thin air deep into my bronchi, forcing oxygen into every cubic millimeter I could. I held it in for a few seconds, then exhaled, pushing it all out with my abdominal muscles. Genaro had taught us that forcing out all the carbon dioxide was important, making more room for oxygen with the next breath.

I sat quietly on the frigid hard rock, breathing deeply in and out. I watched Matt, hoping he was getting enough oxygen during his nap.

"Check your gear," Genaro reminded us. He had instructed during training that at each break, we should go over our gear to make sure everything was in order. I looked down and pulled on my harness; it was tight and attached. Check. I wiggled my helmet around on my head; it was secure. Check.

I grabbed my sunscreen and reapplied it on my face. Check. I didn't want to forget the sunscreen. The thin atmosphere at high elevation increases the risk of ultraviolet radiation damaging your skin. I went through the rest of my gear. All was in order.

So tired, I started nodding off and struggled to stay awake. To prevent myself from falling asleep, I tried to keep my body and mind active. I moved my feet and legs around to keep them warm and began thinking about breaks I take in my everyday life with brain cancer.

There are times when my brain shuts down and needs a break. After going through brain surgery and radiation, my brain can only handle so much. Multitasking, over stimulation from sounds and movement, and working my memory wear out my mind.

I often have to shut myself away from the world around me, sneak into my bedroom, and close the door and curl up on the bed. If I'm away from home, I shut myself into a bathroom and sit quietly on the toilet.

Matt gave me earplugs, and my mom gave me eye covers so I could withdraw deep into the darkness and complete silence. Another brain tumor survivor told me, it's like we need to hit the Restart button on the computer in our brains. That was definitely true for me.

I have always loved being around my boys and visiting friends. But sometimes I have to sneak away and hide. When I went on school field trips with Grant or Clint, children surrounded me all day. I loved watching them play with the expressions on their faces and the excitement in their eyes. But my brain would get worn down quickly with lots of questions and things the kids wanted to tell me. "Mrs. Broyles, what's this?" "Mrs. Broyles, can you help me?" "Mrs. Broyles, come here, you have to see this!" "Mrs. Broyles, yesterday my dog ran away, have I told you about that?" Often, more than one talked to me at the same time.

The children were so cute, but they didn't understand that part of my brain was missing and part of it was suffering from radiation damage. I looked normal and healthy. Smiling at them, kneeling down to their height, trying hard to give them all the attention they needed. It was always wonderful being around them, but I knew when I got home, I would need to crawl into bed and sleep for hours to recover.

Trying to understand numerous people talking all at once is difficult. Sometimes my brain melts down, and I can't understand what they are saying. It sounds more like the teacher's voice on the Charlie Brown cartoon where you just hear *wa wa, wa wa, wa wa wa*. I see mouths moving, but don't understand the words. That's when I know I need a break.

Silence is beautiful. Stillness is refreshing. A blank, cleared mind is comforting. Resting in God's sovereignty is priceless. I remembered the Bible saying, "Be still before your Lord." That's the kind of break I always need.

I stood up and stretched, raising my arms high above my head and taking another big deep breath. Then I lowered my arms and pulled them behind my back, pushing the air all out. It felt good to relax my muscles and clear my mind. A break is always well worth it. I was ready to go on.

CHAPTER 19

ENERGIZE YOURSELF

Before we got going again, Genaro called out, "Remember, drink and eat something before we head up Misery Hill."

I leaned over and shook sleeping beauty. "Matt, wake up."

I dug into my backpack and pulled out my water bottle and two packs of chocolate energy GU. My stomach was empty, but I wasn't hungry. High elevation took my appetite away. I must have burned thousands of calories climbing for over eight hours up Mount Shasta, but I didn't feel like eating anything; my gut, tight like a ball, felt like it couldn't digest. My mouth was so dry that the granola bar I tried to eat earlier felt like the texture of desert sand. I needed to force something down, or I wouldn't have the energy to make it to the peak.

Good thing I had GU Energy Gel. The smooth creamy chocolate-flavored GU was at least tolerable. GU, a power booster for strenuous physical activity, usually kicks in within fifteen minutes. I don't remember the ingredients other than sugar and caffeine; but whatever it is, it works.

"Here, Matt," I called out and tossed a tube to him. It hit him on the shoulder and bounced to the ground. Matt peeled his eyes open, moaned, and reached over to pick it up. I could tell he was as motivated to eat as I was.

Ripping open the one-ounce package, I slowly squeezed the gel into my mouth. Even though I never felt like eating it when I really needed to, I appreciated its power to invigorate me.

Using my tongue, I smoothed it around my mouth. I tried to relax and get a few more minutes of rest before starting out again. My mind wandered off to other things that invigorated my life during my cancer climb.

ENERGIZE YOURSELF

What I had learned over time was the importance of consciously doing something to energize myself. Doing it routinely, not waiting until my fuel tank was already on empty.

A good laugh is a great energizer. I wish I could store laughs in a tube and squeeze them out when needed. The best laughs come spontaneously, and you never know when they'll come. Ones that hit you deep down in your gut, cutting your breath short and bringing tears to your eyes, big belly laughs that force you to grab your stomach and collapse. They keep going and going until the muscles around your smile burn. To stop the stinging smile, I have to push the sides of my mouth together and massage my cheeks. I do have to say, the cheek pain is well worth it!

I've actually gotten some pretty good laughs out of what we brain tumor survivors call "tumor humor." After brain surgery and radiation, it seems like things get "miss-wired." I often forget words or use the wrong ones (called aphasia).

One night, at the kitchen table, I told Grant, "Eat your booger."

Grant started laughing and stuck his finger deep in his nose and began digging around, trying to find one. It's always a few seconds later that I realized a wrong word came out.

"I mean your burger, Grant." We all laughed.

When I feel my fuel tank is running low, I search for something to energize myself—listening to my favorite songs, watching funny movies, playing card games with my boys, or just wrestling with my dog. Grant and Clint love it when I turn on classic rock and roll, and we dance in circles around the living room while singing and laughing. I often hear, "Mom, you're funny."

Matt and I also love to load up our four-wheel drive truck with the boys, our dogs, and lunch, then head to the woods—especially in the winter when mountains are covered with snow and we have a Stanley thermos full of hot chocolate. There are laughs and screams of joy when we slide uncontrollably down the hill on snow sleds, laughing even harder when someone falls off and is buried deep in the white powder.

The family camping – Summer 2001

Beyond laughing, the Bible is my true GU in life. Back when I was going through the last phases of my radiation at home, I was whipped. Radiation, like a parasite, sucked out my energy. I felt like a wet limp washrag. During the weeks of radiation, I was still cleaning house, paying bills, feeding our pets, and being a wife and mommy. This meant I changed diapers, gave baths, fed, played with, and kept an eye on the energetic kids. At one and three, Grant and Clint couldn't be left unattended.

They had so much energy I couldn't keep up. "Mommy, let's play." "Mommy, I'm hungry." "Mommy, hold me." I would hear over and over. I often felt like I couldn't lift a finger, let alone keep up with two boys. Like the Energizer Bunny, they kept going and going and going and going.

Matt could only help so much; he needed to be at work Monday through Friday. In the afternoon, Matt met me at the hospital and sat in the car watching the boys for fifteen or so minutes, while I went in to get radiated. Afterward, Matt usually took Grant to preschool at church for the rest of the day, while Clint and I headed home for our afternoon naps. We'd curl up in bed together and sleep for hours until Matt came home from work with Grant.

During that time, I was repeatedly amazed by how powerful God's GU was. One moment, I felt like curling up in a fetal position and hibernating, then after reading God's Word, I felt like I was given enough energy to get up and move on.

Sometimes it only took one verse, like 2 Corinthians 12:9, "My grace is sufficient for you, for my power is made perfect in weakness." And I felt energized. Sometimes I needed a big deep swallow of a whole chapter. The great thing about God's GU for me is that it doesn't just energize me physically. It boosts my emotions, my courage, my wisdom, my hope, and more.

I was jerked back to the present when I heard Genaro yell, "Let's go! Misery Hill is calling." I stuffed my empty chocolate GU package into my pocket and slowly stood up. I sure didn't feel like the Energizer Bunny, but I had enough energy to keep moving ahead. Our team filed out in line and followed Genaro up the trail.

CHAPTER 20

A LITTLE ENCOURAGEMENT GOES A LONG WAY

At the base of Misery Hill, we stopped and stared. The intimidating gravelly slope was so steep. Switchback after switchback twisted its way up. It looked like it would live up to its name.

I took a deep breath and slowly let it out. Brandon must have noticed my discouragement. He walked over and stood next to me. Looking at Misery Hill, he said, "You will make it. You're not turning back now, you made it this far." Putting his hand on my shoulder, he continued, "I knew from when I first saw you, you'd make it."

I smiled, but wasn't convinced he was being sincere. I turned to Matt to see if he agreed, but only got a weak smile. He didn't have much energy either.

Genaro started up the switchbacks of Misery Hill, and we all followed him. The rocks were different from what we'd seen lower down the mountain. They were abrasive pea-sized perforated volcanic rocks. A mixture of grays and reds—like rocks you'd see in a gas BBQ grill, but ground into smaller pieces. With each step, they crunched and rolled under my boots like marbles. To stay balanced, I had to focus on each step.

Almost at the peak, I thought I'd get a second wind, an extra boost. Instead it felt like the wind had been knocked out of me, and the distance to the peak felt like miles away.

Misery Hill - it's WAY steeper than it looks.
Climbers can be seen as dark specks near the peak.

At my slow pace, most of the climbers left me behind, except Matt and Brandon. Matt stayed one step ahead of me, and Brandon, one step behind. I was trapped in the middle, forced ahead. If I slowed down, Brandon pushed me along with verbal encouragement.

Even though I couldn't see him back behind me, I heard, "Let's get there," or "You'll never see it if you don't keep moving." If I paused, I'd hear, "Keep going," "Don't stop now," or "Move those feet."

At every tight corner of the switchbacks, if I turned and looked over my shoulder, I would see him smiling. It was so easy for him! As a guide, he climbed Mount Shasta twice a week. I wished I could plug into him and charge my battery.

"You wanna carry me?" I asked, frustrated. He laughed, making me feel even more like a wimp.

If Brandon caught me frowning, he just encouraged me more. He never used many words per sentence, but he never stopped. It must have been his personal goal making sure I hit the summit. His repeated words over and over actually became a mixture of annoyance and amusement at the same time. But I was so worn-out I was ready to give up.

I stopped at a switchback and told Matt, "I can actually see the very tippy top of the peak. That's good enough for me, it's like I am actually there. I'll just sit here and wait for you. You go ahead. Take a picture at the top, and I'll see it when the film's developed."

At that point, it wasn't that I thought I couldn't do it. I was just so tired; the desire was gone. I wanted to lie down and sleep.

That comment gave Matt a second wind, and he responded quickly and with venom. "No way, you are not stopping! You're the one who talked me into making this climb. You've come too far not to make it to the very top. Keep going, NOW!" It was more of a command than a request.

At that point, Matt and Brandon started playing team tag. Matt encouraged me from the front, and Brandon reassured me from the back. They acted like mountaineering cheerleaders. But if I told them so, I'm sure they would have kicked me back down the mountain.

Matt knew how much I'd regret it if I didn't actually kneel down and touch the mountain's peak. If I failed, I would pressure him to make the climb again the next year. "I will never ever, ever make this climb again with you, Cheryl. You better keep moving!" He kept pushing me with his harsh style of encouragement.

Brandon and Matt continued tag teaming, and it actually got funny. "OK, fine! I'll do it," I said, and I couldn't help but laugh. However, it actually didn't really sound like a laugh, more like a moan. I was so tired, but I sucked it up and moved forward.

Encouragement can be like magic, seeping in, moving through me, and pushing me ahead. It kept moving me forward when I stopped at each switchback on my trial through brain cancer.

One of the first nudges after being diagnosed was a book I read. After picking it up, I never set it down. Lance Armstrong's *It's Not About the Bike* motivated me. He, too, was battling cancer, fighting his way through it. He never gave up. He kept on riding his bike. As things got worse, he just pushed himself harder. What an inspiration. He set such a great example. After reading his book, I started running and biking. I kept moving and moving. Just like Lance, I was not going to stop. Ever.

Encouragement came from the left and the right. When first diagnosed, Dr. Delashaw advised me to go home, live, and enjoy my life. He told me, "Don't pay attention to statistics. You're not a number." I left his office with hope.

On the Internet, I met many others with glioblastomas. Often their mountains were higher, steeper, and uglier than mine. Still, they urged me on. I'd hear, "Don't give up" or "Keep fighting until they find a cure," and often, "You can enjoy life, even with cancer."

Some people reassured me with a look in their eyes. No words were needed. A tight hug or a squeeze on my hand provided optimism in silence.

Sometimes I even cheered myself. "If anyone can do it, I can," I'd say as I slid into the MRI machine. "I'm strong, I can beat it," I'd say after hearing about another friend with brain tumor passing away. "I'll set a new record," I'd exclaim after reading gloomy research about brain tumor patients' life expectancies.

It surprises me when friends and family thank me and say, "When I have a hard day, I think of how strong you are, and it encourages me to move on." Friends I met on the Internet who have just been diagnosed with brain tumor tell me, "When I read statistics that I would most likely die in a year, I think about you surviving four, and it gives me hope." It's neat to hear how my life affects others. It inspires me to excel and move on.

Encouragement also comes from memories of someone who is no longer with me. My uncle Robie got his wings and flew to heaven when he was only twenty-one years old. I was five at the time. He had Duchenne's muscular dystrophy. By kindergarten, he was stumbling and falling. By six, he was in a wheelchair. Doctors said, "He will never live to adulthood." That never slowed him down, spiritually. My time with him was spent sitting on his lap. That was all we could do because he was paralyzed from the chest down. He was able to move his arms and hands and would hold me tight. My uncle Robie has inspired me since I was a child, a teen, an adult, and, especially, when I was diagnosed with cancer. During his life, he wrote poems that hearten all who read them. One I love, he wrote when he was just a child.

Cheryl's Uncle Robie

A Boy in a Wheelchair

I can't help but wonder dear Jesus
While I am so tired in this wheelchair,
How would it feel to run and play?
Not to have to sit by the wayside always looking on,
To be like the other children and join them in their fun.

Oh well, in my books I can go anywhere.
Doesn't really matter, in a moment I'll be there.

A LITTLE ENCOURAGEMENT GOES A LONG WAY

In my mind I hear a whisper;
I would really like to hear them say,
"Gee, Robie, that was a beautiful home run you hit today."

Like Lazarus in the days of old
Someday God will set me free.
He will break the chains that bind me
"Arise, my child, come unto me."

Today you will take me home?
I can see the gates of heaven
The streets all paved with gold.

Maybe when I get to heaven
I'll be too old to run and play.
But maybe God will let me for a moment,
Just see how it feels anyway.

Thank you for the glimpse of heaven, Lord
And all the wonders there.
For I won't need a wheelchair in heaven
When I go to live up there.

Uncle Robie always inspired me, a paralyzed boy willing to climb a challenging mountain in a wheelchair. He taught me to keep going, even when it seems impossible.

Encouragement also comes from things that surround me daily—a beautiful sunset, a breeze caressing my hair, singing of sweet birds, and laughs from the mouths of children.

Even though they are there for me every day, sometimes I miss them. They pass by unnoticed. Now, after learning, I try to keep my eyes and ears open and alert to catch them all.

As Matt and Brandon continued team-tag encouragement, I proceeded to climb. Up and up through Misery Hill I went.

CHAPTER 21

NOTICE THE MIRACLES

The last climb to the peak

We finally reached the top of Misery Hill. I leaned over, pressing my hands on my knees, closing my eyes, and taking deep breaths. I was exhausted.

Slowly, I opened my eyes, lifted my head, and saw there was only forty feet to go. My lips broke into a smile, and a laugh whispered out.

The last little bit of the climb was up through large boulders stacked on one another, creating what looked like a small Egyptian pyramid. Straightening up, I automatically stepped forward, my hands grasping and pulling on the large stones, my feet digging in and pushing.

During the last few feet of the climb, I noticed IT—divine intervention. I never would have made it to the peak on my own. From the beginning to the end of the climb, there was a marvel about it. It was a miracle.

Miracle after miracle that had happened in my life with cancer rushed through my mind as I pulled and pushed myself up through the boulders.

Before being diagnosed, I didn't believe miracles still happened. I felt they were only real in biblical times; when God split the Red Sea for Moses, saved Noah in the ark during the flood, protected Daniel in the lion's den, when Jesus raised the dead and healed the sick. I was doubtful miracles would happen in my life.

After being diagnosed, I began noticing too many wonders to say, "They just happened by chance." Miracles were real. It wasn't just one huge thing that occurred once in my life, but an uncountable number of things, both big and small, that happened almost daily. They were gifts from God.

Large miracles, like surviving four years after being diagnosed with terminal cancer and told I only had a year to live. My glioblastoma tumor was found when only the size of an acorn. Most GBMs aren't found until the size of a golf ball, after causing a seizure, paralyzing an arm, or after losing sight or speech—often, after the tumor invaded the brain and surgery was no longer possible.

My tumor was found early because it was mixed into the cluster of leaking arteries and veins (AVM), an extremely rare combination. My neurosurgeon told me he'd never seen it before. The AVM bled, causing a headache, which allowed us to catch the tumor early. I remember my nurse telling me, "You're very lucky." I don't believe in luck. It was a miracle.

Small miracles happened too, almost daily. Like when we moved from our thirty-two acres of forestland to a small lot in town. Moving to the new house in the late fall, I didn't notice the miracle until the next spring. As the front yard tree leafed out, I noticed it was a tulip tree. A tree I always hoped to have one day. God knew I lost a forest, but gave me the gift of one tree I'd dreamed of, the one that would fit in my small front yard. Out of all the types of trees that could have been planted there in the past, what's the chance it just happened to be the tree I'd dreamed of? It wasn't just luck. It was a miracle.

It's important not to miss the miracles, like missing other beautiful and meaningful little things. Like walking through a meadow, blinking my eyes, and missing the view of a hummingbird flying by. Like driving along the road, glancing in the review mirror, and missing the sight of a good friend waving as I drove by. I don't want the little miracles passing by unnoticed. I want to see them and enjoy the gifts.

Climbing the last few feet to the peak, I was overwhelmed with the appreciation of miracles. Miracles don't happen out of luck or by chance. They are gifts.

You've got to believe, look; then you'll see.

CHAPTER 22

IN A BLUR

A few steps away from the top, it all became a blur. I sank down against a rock, about ten feet away from what is considered the peak. There the U.S. Forest Service has a book for visitors to sign, to document your official arrival.

I melted into the stone and didn't move. My surroundings became a blur, and I spaced out. In the periphery of my sight, there was movement and excited voices, but I couldn't see or hear it clearly.

Matt sat down beside me and put his hand on my knee. "We're here, Cheryl. Aren't you glad? You made it! Get up, look around." I didn't move or talk to him. It was all a blur.

I knew I had made it to the top, but was too tired to celebrate. I just sat there. I couldn't even look around. I just lowered my head into my hands and closed my eyes. I had worked so hard to make it, but at that point, I didn't even really care. After making sure I was warm enough and OK, Matt got up and walked off to experience the view. I sat in silence, recovering. I don't know how much time went by. My mind was blank.

Blank, like when I came out of anesthesia after brain surgery. I heard voices and sounds, but was lost in a fog. I felt something touching me, but where and what I didn't know. My shoulder shook and I heard, "Wake up, wake up. What's your name?" The fog didn't clear. I could see a bright light through my eyelids, but didn't want to open them. Again, my shoulder shook. I opened my eyes. Someone was standing beside me, but I didn't know who and didn't care. "What is your name?"

"Cheryl," I said, feeling my way through the fog, trying to find her. "Cheryl, Cheryl," I said, but didn't know where she was. After surgery, I was in a blur for days. Slowly, very slowly, I found her. Slowly, the blur cleared.

Since surgery, I've been lost in big loud crowded places—at busy grocery stores, at movie theaters, at church on Sunday, or at the county fair. The noises and movements surround me. After surgery and radiation, my mind just can't handle it all at once. My mind falls—or escapes—into a blur. It's like I'm seeing through water, looking out from within a fish tank. Sounds are garbled; they all rush together. I have to sit down and close my eyes. Whenever it happens to me, I keep searching through the fog until I find myself. It takes awhile for it all to clear. I've learned I need to patiently wait awhile. It will clear. When my sight comes back into focus, I often realize my view is clearer than it ever was before.

Cheryl, thumbs up for reaching the peak

IN A BLUR

I felt someone shaking my shoulder. Was I coming out of surgery? I lifted my head out of my hands and opened my eyes. It was Matt. *That's right; we are at the peak of Mount Shasta.* The blur cleared and my mind focused. I took a deep breath.

"Cheryl, we're going to leave soon to head back down. You need to get up and look around. Come on." He was standing there reaching out to me. I smiled, put my hand in his, and he pulled me up.

CHAPTER 23

AT THE PEAK

I got to my feet and looked around. It was breathtaking. Matt and I stood there in silence, taking it all in. I moved slowly in a circle to get the panorama, looking gradually from the north, to the east, to the south, to the west. I was speechless. It was beyond beautiful.

Matt's eyes filled with tears. Mine did too but, for the first time on this climb, out of joy, not anxiety or pain. We both wiped our tears away to see clearly. Matt reached out for my hand and held it tightly.

We could see over a hundred miles in most directions. Mountains and peaks surrounded us. They were colored with pastel pinks, blues, grays, and light greens. We saw the snow-covered pyramid of Mount McLaughlin to the north, the jagged rim of Crater Lake to the northeast, Mount Lassen to the southeast, Castle Crags to the south, and the Pacific Coast Range to the west.

I had planned on celebrating when I got to the peak, raising my arms, and yelling, "I've made it." But I realized it was not needed. No words or actions could fully express what I felt. All I needed to do was stand there and look in awe at God's creation.

Our team gathered around, shaking hands or giving one another big bear hugs. We were so happy. Our team, minus one, had made it to the peak, seven out of eight—87.5 percent. We beat the statistics, which predicted only 33 percent. After we congratulated one another, I walked over to the edge. I leaned against a boulder and looked out at the grandeur.

I felt so strong deep inside my soul. *I can persevere through any challenge.* My eyes got teary again when the realization hit me. *After this experience, my life will never be the same.* I was rejuvenated, able to see life anew. It wasn't the view at the summit that changed me, but the hard work I did to get there. The experience on the way there shaped my view from the peak. It's what sprang out the grandeur of it. That view could never have been seen from any other place in the world.

I took out my camera and snapped pictures in all directions, though I knew the photos would never capture the fullness on film. No one could look at the pictures and witness or experience what I did unless they had climbed the mountain themselves.

I remembered growing up taking numerous pictures of Half Dome, Nevada Falls, and El Capitan at Yosemite National Park, getting home and being so disappointed when they were developed. The photos only captured a small portion of the beauty. *Oh well, it will always be in my memory.*

Matt and Cheryl at the peak.

My thoughts evaporated when I heard, "Here, Cheryl, give me your camera." Brandon held out his hand. "I'll get a picture of you two." Matt and I sat down on a rock. He put his arm around my back, and we both smiled. Click. That was a picture we would treasure.

"Let's head out," Genaro called. I pulled my pack up on my shoulders. It felt ten times heavier than before. Later that day, I realized I never signed my John Hancock in the visitor's book. *That's OK, the experience has been burned in my memory, and that signature can never be erased.*

CHAPTER 24

BACK DOWN THE MOUNTAIN

We gathered our gear and got ready for the descent. I wondered if going down was any easier than climbing up. I hoped so. At least I'd hit the climax. Maybe gravity would just pull me back down to the car. What was the saying? Something like, a horse moves twice as fast back to the barn as it does heading out. Well, Genaro was leading us back to Horse Camp, so maybe I would experience the same effect.

My legs were still so sore, I was worried they would buckle and I'd collapse. I found out a few minutes later they weren't needed much for the trip back down.

Genaro gathered the group together. "We can go down the same way we came up, or take a different route." We glanced at one another, wondering what route number 2 looked like. "There is a way down that's faster, but we'd need to belay down through a crevice between two rocks, about a fifteen-foot drop. We have the equipment to do it, but there are risks. Just because we're at the peak doesn't mean the risks and hard work are over."

"How much time would we save?" someone asked.

"Hours," Genaro responded. We all voted for the quick way.

"OK, let's go." We climbed down through the boulders off the peak. Sliding through the marble-shaped stones of Misery Hill, and then pounding our knees repeatedly on Red Banks, we finally got to the place where we would work around to the east of the Heart by belaying down through a narrow slit between two large rocks.

Genaro and Brandon set up the ropes and gear. Brandon sat at the top with the rope wrapped around his waist; his feet anchored against solid rock holding tension on the rope. One at a time, each of us attached our carabineer to the rope and rappelled through the long slender crack. Brandon free-climbed down to join us.

At the bottom of the crevice, we turned to Genaro for instructions on the next step. "Now we get to have some fun!" he said. "We're going to glissade down the mountain in icy chutes. We can make it down that way ten times faster than climbing up." We were all excited and ready for that.

"You sit on your behind, hold your ax to the side, and drag it in the ice to keep your speed under control. If you get going too fast, you could end up breaking a leg or impaling yourself with the ax."

Genaro took his backpack off and pulled out a heavy smooth, flexible blue plastic sheet shaped like an hourglass. "I brought this to experiment with. My plan is that it will help me go faster, but more importantly, it will save my rear end and the back of my pants." He told us there were rocks in the chute and chunks of ice that could bruise our posterior and could rip our mountaineering pants.

Genaro straddled the skinny part of the hourglass and pulled up the front and back like a diaper. He tied it in place with a thin rope. We all grinned, not sure if we wished to have one of the plastic sheets or not. Judgment would be reserved until Genaro gave us a performance. Maybe he would plunge down the chute out of control in his homemade toboggan diaper so we could get a good laugh at his expense.

Deborah, the California police officer, stepped forward and said she would go first. She had a great attitude the whole climb to the peak. Confident in herself, she jumped quickly into the chute. Unfortunately, she accidentally toppled to her side, not in the proper position to use the ax to slow down. She slid like a bullet, finally slowing down and stopping when she hit a small level area. From a long distance upslope, we held our collective breath, wondering if she was OK. After a moment, she stood up and waved to us. We all let out our breath and laughed.

"My turn now," Genaro said. "Let's see how this works." He carefully lowered himself into the chute, making sure he was aligned straight and upright, then took off. Sitting up straight, he carved his ax into the ice and was able to control his speed. After seeing the proper technique, we each took turns sliding down the steep slope. I was one of the last to get into the chute, after observing enough to feel confident.

Off I went, grinding the ax into the ice. I quickly hit the speed you get while sliding down a huge waterslide at an amusement park. The rocks and ice were mean and hard. "Ouch! Ouch! Ouch!"

I called over and over as my fanny hit rock or hard ice the whole way down. It hurt, but it was fun.

When we got to the bottom of the first track, James who always seemed to have a smile on his face had completely ripped out the backside of his thin nylon Windbreaker pants. We all laughed with him. He took a shirt from his backpack and tied it around his waist and through his legs like a diaper. What we needed was a pillow to cushion our butts as we banged and scraped over rock after rock.

Partway down the mountain, we passed by Lake Helen again. That time of day, mid-afternoon, it looked completely different. All but a few of the tents were gone. In their place were tent-sized pits in the snow, three to four feet deep. Climbers who camped there the night before had been hours ahead of us to the peak. They already had been back to break camp and head down. The pits may have been dug with shovels in order to create shelter spots for the tents or may have been spots melted by warm sleeping bodies every night during the climbing season. With the tents missing, the large pits looked like the moon's cratered surface.

We continued down the slope. Over an hour later, down chute after chute, my hind end was frozen, numb, and bruised. Glissading had pushed my underwear and pants right up my butt crack, causing a serious wedgie. My butt, clothing, and fingers were so frozen, so I had to mine like a prospector to dig my underwear out. I didn't care if anyone saw me digging; I was sure they all had the same problem.

At the bottom of the chutes, the ground leveled out. There was less-than-a-mile hike back to Horse Camp on a snow-covered path. We had separated by that point—some rushing ahead to camp; others taking it slow, walking awkwardly with butt damage. I walked like a penguin. Genaro and Brandon brought up the back, making sure no one was left behind.

On our way out, we saw others just starting their climb up. That night, they would be camping at Lake Helen. Just like others encouraged me on my way up, I encouraged them. I often heard the same question: "Was it worth it?" I would always say, "Yes—keep going!" I hoped they could see a sparkle in my eyes.

We eventually got to camp and took down the tents. It had taken us ten hours to make it to the peak and less than three to make it back down to Horse Camp. It felt like days. We took down the tents, gathered the gear together, and headed back to the trailhead. After being above the tree line all day, walking through the forest was like being in a tunnel of thick green canopy.

Coming out of the forest, we stepped on to the pavement in the parking lot. It felt so odd and stiff after climbing and hiking through the ice and rocky ground all day. We dropped our gear and stretched. Feeling close like family, we gave one another hugs and exchanged addresses, even though we knew we would probably never talk again. But it felt good to make the effort.

Genaro told us all to gather close on the big log near the trailhead so he could take the "after" picture. He had hoped to have all eight of us there, but seven out of eight beat the statistics. Click. We got up and headed out to our cars, waving good-bye as we separated. Matt and I climbed into the van, sat back, and breathed a sigh of relief. It was over. We did it!

We had reserved a room in the little town of Mount Shasta at the base of the mountain. We'd been told it was the best hotel in town. Driving off, we looked forward to relaxing and taking a nice hot shower.

CHAPTER 25

IT NEVER ENDS

Driving down the curvy mountain road, I can't believe the first things I said, "What about climbing Mount Whitney next summer?" Had I already forgotten how much pain I'd been in? I guess it is the same when women chose to have a second baby. The pain can end with a sweet result that made it worth it.

Matt had been motivated enough too and said, "That is a beautiful mountain. We could do that."

We pulled into the hotel parking lot around seven that evening. Still dressed in hiking clothes, we smelled horrible. We decided it didn't matter and headed straight over to a Mexican restaurant next door. We hadn't eaten that day except for tubes of GU and energy bars. A chicken enchilada, tostada, and taco sounded wonderful. My stomach growled in anticipation.

We were seated quickly and ordered right away. My mouth watered when the waiter served me. The plate was still steaming. Loads of melted cheese covered the refried beans and enchilada. The lettuce and tomatoes on the tostada and taco looked crisp and fresh. I picked up my fork, ready to take my first bite. All of a sudden, I was overcome with nausea and thought I was going to throw up. The food smelled and looked great, and I wanted it so badly, but I couldn't take a bite. Coming down from high elevation quickly can make you sick, and I guess that's what happened. I pushed away my plate and watched with envy as Matt ate.

Taking my eyes off his plate, I started thinking about a hot shower. I started to shiver. My body must have thought I was still in freezing ice. The restaurant was warm, in the seventies, but my body was off-kilter. It shook. I didn't feel well at all. I started dozing, my head nodding. Matt ate as fast as he could, paid the bill, and we left for the hotel.

Once in the hotel room, I told Matt, "Dibs on the first shower!" I stripped off my clothes as fast as I could. I decided I wasn't up for a long hot shower, just a quick one, then right to bed.

I turned on the water, cranked it to hot, and stepped into the shower. The water was freezing, but I expected it to be hot within seconds. In a hurry, I soaked myself from head to toe. The water never got hot, or even warm. It was a nightmare.

I turned off the water and started shivering uncontrollably. My teeth chattered, and I yelled, "Maaaaaaaatt! There's no hot water!"

Matt rushed in. "Let me check it out." He moved the handle around, like I hadn't tried that already. He had no magic; the water stayed cold.

I lost it. I won't even document what I said. Matt rushed out of the hotel room over to the front desk. I got out of the shower and wrapped a towel around myself, then curled up on the little couch. The bed was calling to me, but I stunk worse than a wet dog. I didn't want to stink up the bed. Still shaking and freezing, I felt like I was going to pass out from exhaustion and hypothermia. I needed some hot water to warm up my body. I seriously began to feel like I should call 911.

Matt returned a short time later and told me the pilot light had blown out, and the hot water tank for the whole building had gotten cold. It would take over an hour for it to warm up. "I CAN'T WAIT THAT LONG!" I screamed, hoping everyone in the whole hotel could hear me.

I started crying. Things kept getting worse and worse. Hadn't I already drained out all my tears climbing up Mount Shasta? Didn't I deserve a nice warm shower? Tears kept coming.

There was a knock at the door.

The front desk lady, a very petite Asian woman with broken English and a heavy accent said, "You come over my office, take shower."

"You've got to be kidding!" I yelled from the couch. "I want my money back NOW!" I was livid, ready to strangle her.

Matt stepped outside with her and closed the door. He knew I was about to attack her, and he was trying to control the situation. He argued with her and pressured her to return our money so we could find another hotel with hot water.

She said she couldn't return our money. "Wait for water," she argued. Obviously, she had never climbed Mount Shasta;

otherwise, she would have taken pity on us. She could tell a bomb was about to explode, so she turned and left.

A few minutes later, she returned. There was a quick *knock, knock, knock.* Matt opened the door, stepped outside, and closed it behind him. A minute or two later, he stepped back in and said, "Get up. Let's go. She got us a room in the hotel across the street. Both hotels are owned by the same person."

I just wanted a hot shower and a bed, so I pulled a jacket over my naked body and crawled into the car. We drove across the street and parked in front of our new hotel room. Matt opened the door, and I rushed to the shower.

The room was a "special room" designed for disabled people. The toilet, shower, lights—everything was set up for them. I jumped into the shower, turned on the hot water, and, sure enough, things got worse.

The showerhead was located at shoulder height, the perfect place for someone in a wheelchair. But it sucked for me! The water came blasting out at my waist. I started laughing, I was beyond crying. Was I going insane? I felt like Gulliver. I had to bend way down to get my head and shoulders wet. Screw cleanliness. I washed off as quickly as I could and went directly to bed. My head hit the pillow, and I was out.

I had just completed the hard climb up Mount Shasta and thought I'd earned and deserved a nice break. But at the hotel, another struggle, up another mountain, hit me in the face.

Does it ever end? No, it never does.

Peaks come in mountain ranges, one right after the other. Some peaks are even located at the top of a volcano that could explode any moment. That's just the way life's geography is. So often we climb up and down, up and down, from peak to peak. Every once in a while we get to stroll peacefully through a smooth green valley. But sure enough, soon you stumble upon another mountain.

Don't expect it to end. It never will.

Here's what's interesting. Some mountains are huge and rarely happen during your life—cancer, divorce, death of a loved one, being raped—like climbing Mount Everest. Some mountains are small, but they seem to happen daily: anger from a disagreement, sadness due to hurt feelings, upset over spilled milk, frustrated because of a flat tire. The small mountains are more like climbing up a kids' slide in a park. You get to the top in eight steps then slide right back down. It's usually quick, and in comparison to the huge ones, it's not so bad. Ones like Mount Everest take days, take all of your attention and strength, and, often, cause a lot of pain.

The ridiculous thing is we usually climb successfully to the peak of *big* mountains, but often fail on the small ones. Like hiking along a trail where we see the big rocks and step over them. It's the tiny pebbles we miss, slip on, and fall upon. Like the minute crack in the cement and the nail faintly protruding from the wooden deck that snags our shoe and trips us.

I made it bravely through brain cancer and climbing Mount Shasta. I stuck with it and gave it my all. But look at the event at the nightmare hotel; I lost it and yelled at a woman when a pilot light blew out. I missed my opportunity to shine, my chance to persevere. Instead, I tripped and fell over a small pebble and yelled in anger as I fell to my face.

I'm not perfect. Life is a journey. It's the small ones I need to work on.

Maybe next time, I can continue stepping over the big rocks and get better at looking for those little pebbles and not trip on them. I could pick them up and carry them with me, rolling them around in my fingers, looking at them and learning. Each life's mountain I climb, I will get stronger and more prepared for the next one coming—big or small.

Two weeks after climbing to the peak of Mount Shasta, another mountain loomed in my horizon. The glioblastoma multiforme returned. My climb started again. In August 2004, I had brain surgery number 2 while awake so my brain could be mapped, then started chemotherapy. The pain of an even larger mountain motivated me to write a book to encourage others climbing their own mountains.

Then, while I was writing the last chapter of this book, January 2007, the GBM came back a third time. Mountains come in ranges. I went for surgery number 3 and started chemotherapy again.

It would take a second book to cover the story of those two mountains! But I will tell you this: I did make the climb to both summits successfully and am ready for any mountain looming in my future.

KOKO. Keep On Keeping On.

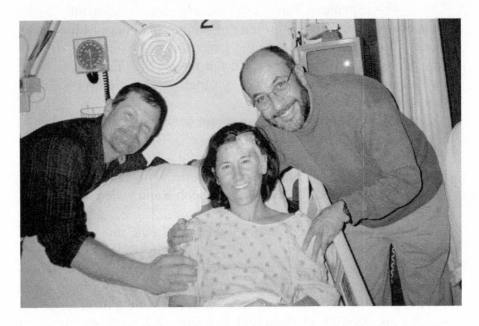

Matt, Cheryl, and Genaro after 2007 surgery

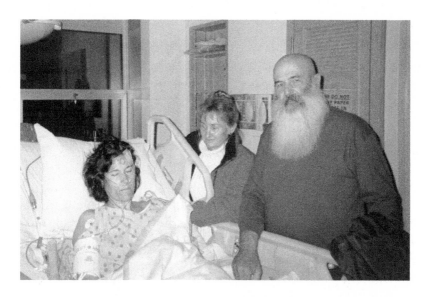

Cheryl, Willy and Ginger after 2007 surgery

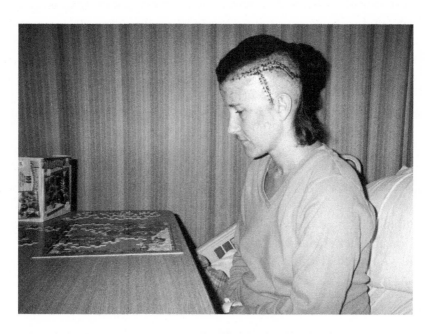

Cheryl after surgery 2007

CHAPTER 26

I'M LEARNING

My story is over, but I want to tell you what I've learned. So many people have helped me in life; now I hope to reach out and help others with encouragement. I don't have all the answers, but I want to share with you what has helped me during my life's mountain climbs. Maybe it could help you too. This is it.

It's OK to keep climbing mountains and peaks, one after the other. It's a blessing. There's a reason we go through each trial—to learn, to grow, to mature, to become a stronger person. Think about it. Look back at some of your climbs. Don't you often see benefits at the end? Sometimes the benefit is a mystery, and you can't clearly see it yet. But it's there. At times you need to look hard. Each "mountain" I've climbed, I've gotten stronger and wiser.

I never thought I would say this: I actually look forward to the climbs. Yes, really. Not that I want to be in pain or suffering, but I want the growth. I want to keep learning. I appreciate it and look forward to it in some weird way. Now that I perceive climbs that way, I'm not as scared as before when I see a new peak in the horizon.

I'm aware in my daily life that growth can occur at anytime. I keep vigilant, looking around for opportunities to grow. If a mountain hits me hard, I don't try to avoid it. I don't want to miss out on the benefits. I climb right up. Climbs hit you at the exact time you need them. Not early, not late. They don't happen by chance.

I believe there is a god. He has a plan for me and you. Things come into our lives with a purpose. God molds us like clay. It may be a mystery to us, but we can be confident there's always a reason.

I used to think I needed XYZ in my life to really enjoy it. Now I know I can enjoy life no matter what happens. The last seven years have been the best of my life, even with cancer. Even though the mountains I've climbed have been huge and a struggle, I've gotten a peace and a feeling of love that is invaluable.

There's more good news. To me, the biggest thing I've learned: Once you accept that the trials are blessings, the good times and bad times become one. The old scars and the new growth combine. The ups and the downs level out and become a golden path of life. One that's always joyful to walk along. At that point, you can love each second of your life and feel happiness no matter what happens.

Matt and I have grown, and our relationship has ripened while we've climbed together. We've learned how to persevere. Grant and Clint, ten and eight years old now, are starting to climb their own mountains. Mom has cancer. They have seen me suffer and know cancer may get me one day. I hope Matt and I have been good guides and that our boys have learned skills from watching their parents climb. I trust they can find their own mountaineering gear and see that God is always there. They will never climb alone.

I'm not going to keep going on and on about this topic. I'll sit back, relax, and get ready for my next climb.

James 1:2-5, 12 "Consider it pure joy, my brothers, whenever you face trials of many kinds, because you know that the testing of your faith develops perseverance. Perseverance must finish its work so that you may be mature and complete, not lacking anything. If any of you lacks wisdom, he should ask God, who gives generously to all without finding fault, and it will be given to him . . . Blessed is the man who perseveres under trial, because when he has stood the test, he will receive the crown of life that God has promised to those who love Him."

CHAPTER 27

A NEW CHAPTER IN LIFE

It's now May 2012.

It's been over three years since *Life's Mountains* was first published, and eleven years since I was diagnosed with the Glioblastoma Multiforme. Most all of the aspects of my life have significantly changed over time, while only one thing has held rock-solid.

My two sons have grown and have become honorable young men. Grant, fifteen, is now as tall as his father, and Clint, twelve years old, has met my height.

Grant, Cheryl, and Clint at Death Valley N.P. 2011

They have lived through the three GBM recurrences with me, each time they seem to have grown stronger and have become more prepared to handle any difficult times that may appear in their lives. The hormones have kicked in and my sons have changed from little boys to young men!

Matt and I have been married 21 years now and we still love life together even though things appear to change daily. In our mid-forties we are starting to feel and look "older". Our boys even tell us so! They definitely notice our gray hair starting to pepper in.

Matt and I have some days when our marriage is so effortless and stimulating. On those days our love seems so high, looking into each others eyes everything else ceases to exist. Unfortunately it's not like that every day. As other things change, so does marriage.

Some days are not so pretty; like when another MRI is coming up, or Matt has a hard time at work and is annoyed, or our two boys are being boys and wrestling and arguing together under my feet, or our roof shingles begin to blow off and the whole roof needs to be replaced, or worst of all for me, I have a "bad brain day".

On those days, Matt and I struggle together. Sometimes it feels like we are butting heads like bighorn sheep slamming their horns together; unfortunately, painful for both of us. Then some days we strengthen each other and amaze ourselves at what we can accomplish together, our love running deeper and stronger than the daily emotional ups and downs the GBM brings. Regardless of the good, the bad and the ugly, we are committed to each other and our marriage.

One thing that often comes to my mind while Matt and I are butting heads is what an old woman said one evening during a neighborhood dinner. A sweet couple was celebrating their 50th anniversary and I said with awe, "You two must truly love each other to stay married for fifty years!"

She smiled and said with oomph, "Yes, I love him every day, but there are some days I don't like him!"

Her husband smiled at her with loving eyes and nodded. I sat there absorbing what she said, taking it in as a very wise proverb.

Marriages are never rock-hard stable. Our feelings about marriage change daily, sometimes hourly, along with our emotions and circumstances in life. But I can't imagine living through those relentless changes in life without Matt by my side.

Our family still loves getting out in nature, camping, backpacking, hiking, hunting, biking, rafting, skiing, anything in the outdoors! What our family has been capable of achieving has changed over time. When our boys were little our family went for smaller nature expeditions, taking short backpacking trips into the woods with mom and dad carrying all the weight. As the boys grew and became stronger, we began planning exciting and more challenging trips! Last summer we backpacked and hiked to the top of Half Dome at Yosemite National Park. Matt, having a fear of heights, had a harder time with the final climb up the cables than the boys! Next summer we plan on something more challenging, a climb to the peak of Mount Whitney at 14,496 feet elevation. I'm excited just thinking about it!

Matt at the cables on Half Dome

What I physically can accomplish outdoors also changes, varying on what my MRI shows and what treatments I'm on. Over time I've learned to weave in the outdoor activities I love, that go along with the physical capabilities I have at that time. For example, during the days I was recovering from my four brain surgeries, I would take mild mountain bike rides along smooth forest trails, rather than the gnarly rocky trails I love, which would have shaken my brain loose! But I still got out moving!

The five days each month I was on Temodar, my big outdoor "expedition" might have just been walking down the level street sidewalk, about 200 feet, to gather our incoming parcels from the mailbox (in my P.J.s) and that was a challenge! Then the weeks following, as I recovered from the Temodar quickly, I would exercise harder each day. Two weeks later I often had the energy to enter races. During the 3+ years I was on Temodar, I competed in a handful of mini-marathons, duathlons (run, bike, run), 5K to 20K runs, x-country ski, and mountain bike races. I never won first place, but I always hit the finish line!

California Redwoods Forest Trail run, 11 miles May 2005

What I can physically accomplish outdoors (or in my house) never seems to stay consistent, but I continue to move all I can, enjoying each peddle, climb, run, hike, swim I can do!

x-country skiing at Crater Lake National Park 2008

Matt & Cheryl at Yosemite NP for Half Dome hike 2011

In 2008 I was able to accomplish something I never thought I would be brave enough to undertake, not physically, but mentally. All due to the blessing of finding out about Inheritance of Hope, a foundation whose mission is to increase the well-being and to help overcome despair in the lives of children and families with a parent diagnosed with a terminal illness. www.inheritanceofhope.org Glioblastoma Multiforme is undoubtedly considered "terminal", so our family qualified and we took an exciting, fully paid for trip, to Disneyworld in Florida for three days. One wonderful and touching blessing they provided was an opportunity to make a legacy video for my boys. In a hotel room they set up a video camera then left me in privacy while I was being videoed giving my two boys my "last" loving words they could listen to after my death. I wanted my boys to remember how much I loved them, what my voice sounded like and my expressions. I never thought I would have the courage to do that and am so thankful that Inheritance of Hope offered the opportunity and encouragement to do it. I left Florida with two DVDs, one for Grant and one for Clint. Hopefully they will not have to view them for many years!

Inheritance of Hope Disney world trip in 2008

Some things that change in my life over time are emotionally painful and come like waves. I make new friends and lose loved friends. Over the internet and at brain tumor conferences and meetings I've been blessed to meet many brain tumor survivors. Because of our similarities living through brain cancer treatments we connect and grow close fast, feeling like family. We reach out supporting and encouraging one another, which is so valuable because we feel no one else really understands what we go through. It seems like weekly my heart is broken as a mourning caregiver gives us notice of a loved one's death. Then over the internet we all grieve together. The gaining and losing of friends is like the never ending ocean waves, the beauty of meeting new friends and the crash of often losing them shortly thereafter. I'm blessed to still be alive, but am often slammed with guilt when I hear about a friends' death. I ask myself over and over again, *why am I alive and they are not?* And I never seem to have an answer. The waves keep coming and change my life repeatedly.

After climbing Mount Shasta in 2004 and publishing Life's Mountains in 2008 I was motivated to create a web page. My heart goes out to everyone battling brain tumors, and I wanted to reach out further to encourage them and to share the lessons I've learned. In 2008 my web page became official at www.cherylbroyles-gbm.com and I never realized it would touch people all over the world. Through my web page I've been blessed to become friends with people from every continent (well not Antarctica), from countries including China, India, Egypt, Canada, Serbia, Brazil, Aruba, New Zealand, Czech Republic, and too many more to list. It's a blessing to feel we are all connected; cheering each other on from all over the world. Then, I stepped out further and joined Facebook and the world got even smaller. Technology and communication change so quickly, I wonder what the future will bring us to experience. It seems to change monthly!

Reaching out with just words was not enough for me; I wanted more. As said, "A picture speaks more than a thousand words." I wanted people to see that a brain tumor survivor can still smile and love life! The scars look ugly after surgery, but we can heal. I needed to put together a video! So in 2009 after my last brain surgery, I put together a video in hopes of connecting with survivors and encouraging them even more. Providing pictures and more pictures, along with words of my climb up Mount Shasta and my life battling brain cancer (neither easy!). http://vimeo.com/22147466 My life keeps changing and never seems to slow down.

The "standard treatment" for Glioblastoma Multiforme has also changed over the last eleven years and the life expectancy for GBM patients has improved. Back in 2000 the standard procedure involved surgery, radiation and a chemotherapy usually used called BCNU. Life expectancy was less than a year, most often three to six months. Now in 2012 there have been changes in all the treatment procedures and the life expectancy has improved! Surgery has changed with new dyes available that help identify cancer cells, giving surgeons the ability to remove many that would have gone unseen in the past. New chemotherapies have been FDA approved (Temodar and Avastin); and even a new electrical magnetic device called Novocure. New and more precise radiation procedures are available now (Gamma Knife, Cyberknife, and proton radiation) taking a step further in treating inoperable brain tumors. Yearly more genetic markers are discovered and tested for; allowing oncologists to better determine which treatments would work best for individual patients (like P53 and EGFR). New clinical trials seem to arise annually with new ideas, such as vaccines specifically designed for the individual patient. So now eleven years after my diagnosis, we are seeing more and more brain tumor survivors lasting over two years and more! These changes are exciting, giving us hope that maybe one day there will be a cure.

Other things that keep changing in my life are my MRIs. Every few months while I'm lying on my back being drawn into the MRI machine, it's a big unknown as to what it will show. The results can be stable, change a little, or change a lot.

In 2004, 2007 and 2009 the MRI showed recurrences with new GBM growth. The first two recurrences were a solid mass located along the perimeter of my tumor cavity in my left temporal lobe. My third recurrence in 2009 the GBM mass was actually not located in my brain itself, but in the meninges which covers over the brain as a protective blanket (the mass still located on the perimeter of my tumor cavity).

I went back into surgery each time, followed by some type of treatment; Temodar twice in 2004 and 2007. I've held steady at taking all of my supplements, eating organic healthful foods, exercising, but after the 2007 surgery I wanted to add something new to my "cocktail" approach of battling brain cancer. I continue to be a more "natural / nature" lover and wanted to avoid hammering my own immune system with more harsh chemotherapy, so I broke down and did something I never thought I would do. It involves many needles!!! Acupuncture. Wow, now after lying peacefully with over twenty needles in my many body parts, I wish I had started it years ago. Relaxing and uplifting, I now get acupuncture two to four times a month. Love it! Things change.

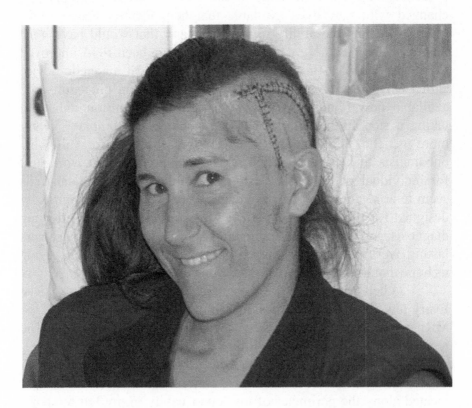

2009 Two days after brain surgery #4 at UCSF

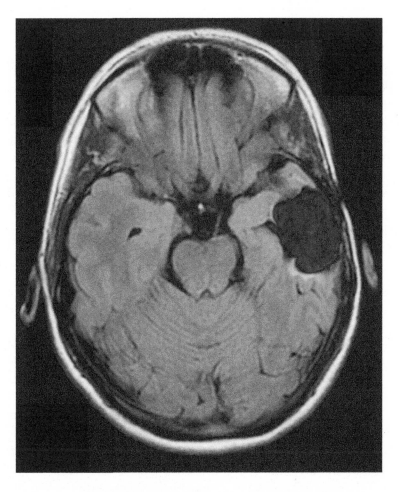

2009 MRI showing tumor cavity

My MRIs have now begun changing in new ways, recently showing more and more radiation damage over time. It's now been eleven years since my conformal radiation, but radiation still keeps doing its job killing brain cells. Small micro-hemorrhages are beginning to appear scattered over my left brain hemisphere. More T2 flair shows up along the perimeter of the tumor cavity, which I'm told is radiation damage. So far, my brain is still functioning (hey I'm still able to write!), but more and more mental challenges crop up as time goes on. As more radiation damage arises, more deficits come along with it. These include a loss of words (mostly nouns), plus a harder time following conversations and comprehending written words. Talking on the phone is hard, multitasking is almost impossible, and my short term memory is vanishing.

In 2010 I was finally tested by a neurophysiologist at UCSF on my cognitive abilities, or lack there of. It showed many of my cognitive abilities controlled by my left temporal lobe were "impaired". However, it was actually comforting that I could better understand were my challenges where and how to compensate for them. I wish I had teamed up with a neurophysiologist years ago!

My emotions and cognitive abilities seem to change daily and sometimes hourly! Some days, unfortunately way fewer days, my brain seems to function exceedingly well, working clearly and quickly. Deficits I have seemed to be milder on those wonderful days. Emotions of cheerfulness come along with those good days. I always wish it could be that way everyday, or that I knew what triggered a good day.

Then there are other days or hours where my brain shuts down and my deficits are significantly more pronounced and difficult. Sometimes I even feel disconnected from my own body, it's hard to describe. On those days everything seems complicated to do, even the simplicity of just taking a shower. Sadness, depression and anxiety come along with those bad brain days.

It's a never ending roller coaster ride of my cognitive abilities and emotions, never stable and never predictable. However, at the end of each day, my brain is usually worn out as if I'd run a mental marathon.

Overall, what I have found in life is that things are always shifting and changing.

•   •   •

There is only one thing that does not change.

One thing that holds rock-solid even when my life shakes and is unstable like moving sand. That is my Lord Jesus Christ. As Hebrews 13:8 tells us "Jesus Christ is the same yesterday and today and forever."

It is Jesus Christ that has held me together, kept me from shattering during the unyielding changes in my life. My Lord always fulfills his promises of salvation, love and hope.

The biggest thing I have become very aware of, that has been so apparent during my eleven years of battling the Glioblastoma Multiforme, is the steadiness of hope, joy and peace I am blessed with through my belief in Jesus Christ.

I can feel happy one day and sad another, all depending on my circumstances. My own mind, its thinking process, is what controls how I "feel", happy or sad. That changes over time.

But the hope, joy and peace I have through Jesus Christ does not alter because I believe. Romans 15:13 explains it so simply, "Now may the God of hope fill you with all joy and peace in believing, that you may abound in hope by the power of the Holy Spirit."

It is the Holy Spirit within me that gives me the power to have hope, joy and peace regardless of the circumstances. I can be told the GBM is back and even though I would definitely be devastated and distressed in the moment, the indescribable peace I have through Jesus Christ comfortably blankets over the sadness.

I am astonished so often by God's consistent and endless love. Over the last eleven years I have learned to have no doubt that Jesus will always be there to hold me together with his mercy and grace.

Just the other day, in the mail, I got my recent MRI radiologist report. I always sit down by myself in quietness to open up the envelope and read the report. My neuro-oncologist told me at UCSF that the MRI looked good, that there was no seen tumor. But I always wait to get the radiologist's report in the mail, to get a second opinion, to confirm the good news.

Reading through the report I got to the "findings" where it describes what the radiologist sees. I read something new that brought back the anxiety and worry about the future. It read, "There are scattered foci of magnetic susceptibility within the left hemisphere, likely to represent micro-hemorrhages due to post treatment changes or radiation induced cavernous malformation." I felt like my breath and heart stopped. *What does that mean?*

Immediately I got on the computer to Google "micro-hemorrhages" and "cavernous malformation" to figure out what was

169

going on in my brain. I know radiation can continue to damage your brain years after the treatment is completed. Of course, in the moment I often think of the worst. Can I have strokes or seizures from the damage? Will I lose my driver's license? Is my brain melting away?

I began to "feel" overwhelmed and beyond sadness. I logged off the computer and sank down onto the couch and began to think. My mind ran all over the place, feeling like a mental earthquake was shaking my emotions. I was about ready to go get my prescription for Ativan, an anti-anxiety medicine that I hold on to for really bad days. This was one.

Then all of a sudden, what came to my mind was what is the most important thing in my life; my Lord Jesus Christ. The verse Hebrews 13:8 jumped out "Jesus Christ is the same yesterday and today and forever."

The thoughts in my mind changed so quickly.

My soul has been saved by Jesus Christ and he never changes. Regardless of the condition of my physical body, my Lord is always there to hold tight to my soul.

I was immediately filled with hope, joy and peace. It felt like I could relax and breathe again. The horrible feeling of doom went away. Peace that surpasses understanding covered me. I am always amazed at how quickly my perspective on life can change when I focus on my Lord. I settled back down comfortably on the couch realizing that I did not need the Ativan after all. Just believing in Christ saves me.

God's word, the Bible, tells us that when we "believe" in Jesus Christ, we are filled with the Holy Spirit which empowers us to do things that on our own we could never achieve. For me, I'm blessed with the power to replace my fear and sadness with hope, peace and joy. I could never do that on my own. So even if the radiation deteriorates my brain and my cognitive ability becomes completely impaired, I can still believe and be sheltered by God's reassuring blanket of hope, peace and joy.

Romans 15:13 keeps telling me, "Now may the God of hope fill you with all joy and peace in believing, that you may abound in hope by the power of the Holy Spirit."

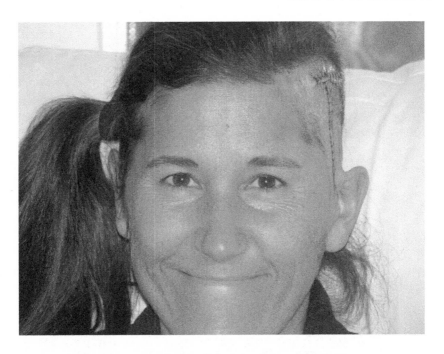

Two days after 2009 brain surgery at UCSF

I am happy to say, I abound in HOPE.
Just believe and you will too.
John 3:16 "For God so loved the world that he gave his one and only son, that whoever believes in him shall not perish but have eternal life."

Cheryl at the top of Half Dome 2011

Made in the USA
Coppell, TX
29 October 2022

85407538R00100